GRILLING WITH BROILMASTER

GOURMET
BARBEQUE
RECIPES

BROILMASTER®
PREMIUM GAS GRILLS

THE MOST DURABLE GRILL
KNOWN TO MAN

Published for

By

 GENERAL STORE
PUBLISHING HOUSE

Box 28, 1694B Burnstown Road, Ontario, Canada K0J 1G0
Telephone (613) 432-7697 or 1-800-465-6072

ISBN 1-894263-33-2

Campbell, Ann, 1948-
    Heaven on a grill cookbook

ISBN 1-894263-33-2

1. Barbecue cookery. I. Title

TX840.B3C33   2001   641.5'784   C00-900590-6

Updated Printing January 2001

Printed in Canada

Thank You!

Congratulations on your purchase of a BROILMASTER®
Premium Gas Grill and thank you for selecting our
product. We hope that your new Broilmaster Premium
Gas Grill will meet your every expectation.

Broilmaster is pleased to provide you with this Gourmet
Barbecue Recipe Cookbook. With built-in features that
allow you to adjust and maintain even, consistent cooking
temperatures, your Broilmaster appliance, will grill,
roast, smoke and even bake virtually any food, including
delicate cakes and breads. We hope it helps refine your
cooking skills and inspires you to create culinary
masterpieces for many years to come. After all, anything
you can cook indoors with your oven or range can be
cooked outdoors with your new Broilmaster Gas Grill.

To enhance your grilling experience and help your grill
stay in top shape, try our Broilmaster Essentials Gourmet
Grilling Accessories available from your dealer.

Thanks again for purchasing a Broilmaster Premium Gas
Grill . . . The Most Durable Grill Known To Man.

**THE MOST DURABLE GRILL
KNOWN TO MAN**

Safe Food Handling Tips

1. Safe Defrosting — *Thawing in the refrigerator* is a safe way to thaw foods slowly. Make sure thawing juices do not drip on other foods. *Thawing in cold water* is faster. Place food in a leak-proof plastic bag and submerge in cold tap water. *Thawing in the microwave* is fastest. Cook meat and poultry immediately after microwave thawing.

2. Keep Everything Clean — Wash hands thoroughly before and after handling raw meat and poultry. Sanitize cutting boards often in a solution of 1 teaspoon chlorine bleach in 1 quart water. After cutting raw meats, wash hands, cutting boards, utensils and counter tops with hot soapy water.

3. Keep Foods Separate — Don't cross contaminate. Keep raw meat, fish and poultry away from other foods in your grocery shopping cart and in your refrigerator. Never place cooked food on a plate which previously held raw meat, poultry or seafood. If some of your marinade is to be used as a sauce on cooked food, reserve a portion of the marinade and don't put raw meat and poultry in it. Don't re-use the marinade used on raw meat or poultry unless it's boiled first to destroy any bacteria.

4. Cook to the Right Temperature — See the chart on the next page.

5. Refrigerate Promptly — Cold temperatures keep harmful bacteria from growing and multiplying. Refrigerate or freeze perishables, prepared foods and leftovers within two hours or less. Never defrost at room temperature, and always marinate foods in the refrigerator.

Safe Cooking Temperatures

Type of Meat: *Cook to Internal Temperature of:*

GROUND MEATS
- Hamburger .... 160°F
- Beef, veal, lamb, pork .... 160°F
- Ground chicken or turkey .... 165°F

BEEF, VEAL, LAMB
Roasts & Steaks
- Medium-rare .... 145°F
- Medium .... 160°F
- Well-done .... 170°F

PORK
Chops, roasts, ribs
- Medium .... 160°F
- Well-done .... 170°F
- Ham, fresh .... 160°F
- Sausage, fresh .... 160°F

POULTRY
- Chicken, whole & pieces .... 180°F
- Duck .... 180°F
- Turkey (unstuffed) .... 180°F
  - Whole .... 180°F
  - Breast .... 170°F
  - Dark meat .... 180°F
  - Stuffing (cooked separately) .... 165°F

FISH .... 140°F

Information provided by USDA and FDA publications.

TABLE OF CONTENTS

Drinks

Fish

Meat

Poultry

Salads

Sandwiches

Vegetables

Understanding Your Broilmaster® Gas Grill

Your ownership of a BROILMASTER Gas Grill opens the door to a new outdoor cooking experience.

It is likely that much of the cooking formerly done with your range and oven in the kitchen will now be done outdoors on your BROILMASTER Grill. Why? Because this gas grill, with its adjustable flame control and wide range of cooking temperatures, has almost unlimited versatility. It can be used for surface cooking or rotisserie cooking. It grills, bakes, or cooks by a combination of the three. Perhaps most important of all . . . meats, fish, fowl and other foods grilled on a BROILMASTER Grill have that wonderful, tangy, smoky flavor formerly associated with charcoal grilling and open pit barbecuing.

"Charcoal Flavor" Without Charcoal?

The now widely recognized truth is charcoal is odorless and flavorless. If you have ever lit a charcoal fire, you know it burns without smoke or aroma until you start cooking. The so-called "charcoal flavor" is imparted to the meat or food by the smoke and flames resulting from the dripping of juices on the hot coals. A gas grill creates this same delicious, smoky flavor by the same process. Instead of charcoal, Charmaster™ naturally cured clay briquets are heated in the gas flames to provide the hot coals.

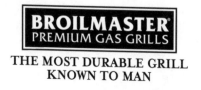

BROILMASTER®
PREMIUM GAS GRILLS

**THE MOST DURABLE GRILL
KNOWN TO MAN**

YOUR BROILMASTER® GIVES YOU COMPLETE COOKING CONTROL

If you have been using a charcoal grill for your outdoor cooking in the past, you will probably go through a short period of "getting used to" your gas grill. But you will soon find that your gas grill offers several important advantages. You not only avoid the work, expense and mess of charcoal, but you gain much more accurate control of cooking results. With a BROILMASTER Premium Gas Grill, you can accurately control cooking temperatures, for any length of time, by one or more of these methods.

1. Adjusting the gas burner valve to any setting between HI and LO (infinite adjustment).

2. Lowering the grill lid to one of three heights above the cooking surface or closing completely (for maximum cooking temperature).

3. Positioning the cooking grids at different levels or angles above the Charmaster™ clay briquets.

4. Changing the low flame setting.

BASIC OPERATING INSTRUCTIONS

1. INITIAL LIGHTING

Read instructions in your owner's manual and follow the directions on the grill before lighting.

(a) With the grill lid open, push and turn the burner control knob counter-clockwise to "HI."

(b) Depending on your model's type of Piezo ignitor, either push the button or turn the knob 3 or 4 times until burner lights.

(c) If burner fails to light after 5 seconds, turn it off for 5 minutes, allowing the gas to clear. Then try the procedure again.

(d) Match lighting may also be done by inserting a long wooden match into the lighter hole and then turning the burner control knob to "HI."

2. PREHEATING GRILL

Before cooking, always preheat the grill a few minutes on "HI" burner setting with the lid closed. This gives the Charmaster™ clay briquets time to heat up in the gas flames. Hot coals mean better, quicker cooking and better flavor.

Caution: Don't leave the grill operating on "HI" burner setting and the lid closed for longer than 30 minutes.

If you are not ready to cook after preheating the grill, raise the lid and use a lower burner setting.

3. POSITIONING THE COOKING GRIDS

The cooking grids for most BROILMASTER Gas Grills may be placed in both level and tilted positions.

The tilt positions are used mainly for the purpose of draining grease faster into a grease receptacle when cooking meats of high fat content.

The lowest level grid position will accommodate quick searing without cooking meats throughout, for "rare" degree of doneness. Higher levels of cooking grids allow for slower cooking, for more "well-done" dishes.

VARIOUS WAYS TO COOK WITH YOUR BROILMASTER®

1. SURFACE GRILLING WITH LID RAISED.

   This method of grilling exposes only the bottom of the meat or food to cooking temperatures. It is the slowest method of cooking on a gas grill, and is therefore suitable only for foods that cook quickly — like bacon, hot dogs, fish fillets, thin steaks or chops, hors d'oeuvres, shish-kabobs, etc.

   People who don't particularly care for a smoky flavor may prefer this method because it provides the least "barbecue" taste. For obvious reasons, it is not a good method when the weather is cold or windy.

2. SURFACE GRILLING WITH LID LOWERED (OR CLOSED COMPLETELY)

   There's no question — you get more flavor when you grill or cook with the lid of your BROILMASTER Gas Grill lowered or closed completely. Therefore, this is by far the most popular method of cooking among BROILMASTER users.

   Meats and foods cook more quickly when the lid is lowered, because heat is confined in the grill and both the top and bottom surfaces of the meat or food are exposed to cooking temperatures.

   You get more flaming and more smoke, and therefore more smoky flavor — but you have to be careful, or you will over-char and over-cook the food. When grilling hamburgers or steaks, most users will use the HI setting — particularly if they like their meat rare or medium. This method insures quick searing and charring of the outside surface without overcooking the center of the meat.

Your own experience will quickly acquaint you with this method of cooking, so you will know what burner settings will produce the cooking results you want, and whether to close the lid completely or prop it open a bit.

3. ROASTING, BAKING OR BARBECUING

By closing the lid of your BROILMASTER Gas Grill you can also make it an oven. By means of burner adjustment and the heat indicator, you can control the temperature inside the grill and use it to bake, roast or barbecue a great variety of foods. For example, you can bake potatoes and vegetables in the closed grill, and then keep the potatoes hot on the warming rack while grilling the steaks, hamburgers or whatever!

4. HUGGA-RACK/ROTISSERIE GRILLING

The most popular accessory for BROILMASTER Gas Grill is the patented Deluxe "Hugga-Rack"™.

It comes complete with Hugga-Grids (that can handle whole turkeys and hams) and a flat basket (great for fish and chicken pieces). A standard rotisserie is available for each BROILMASTER. Either makes rotisserie grilling on your BROILMASTER a great cooking method and offers the following advantages:

   a. Meats brown and cook evenly on all exposed surfaces.

   b. Rotisserie-grilled foods do not require constant attention.

   c. Whole turkeys, hams, and large roasts can be cooked or barbecued with delicious results.

   d. Exact degree of doneness can be easily determined by use of a meat thermometer.

WHETHER TO ROTISSERIE GRILL WITH THE GRILL LID RAISED OR LOWERED?

Meats cooked on a Hugga-Rack or rotisserie with a lower burner setting and the grill lid lowered, will usually be more tender and have a more smoky flavor. This method of cooking exposes the meat to a combination of grilling and baking. It is an outstanding and flavorful way to cook meat and fowl!

5. CLOSED LID GRILLING OR BAKING

Many outdoor cooking enthusiasts use this method most of the time. They like the smoke and flames and the extra smoky flavor it produces.

Many backyard chefs grill steaks (preferably thick), chops and hamburgers with the burner on "HI" setting and grill lid completely closed.

This method produces quicker cooking, smoky flavor and more browning of the meat. It is particularly effective in preparing rare steaks or chops, because it quickly sears and browns the outside of the meat while leaving the inside appetizingly rare.

For slower cooking the burner should be at a lower setting. A combination of a lower burner setting and partially raised lid will produce cooking temperatures in the 300°F to 400°F level needed for slow cooking or grilling. Slow cooking ensures maximum tenderness and less shrinkage of all kinds of meat and fowl.

Used as an oven, your BROILMASTER Gas Grill achieves marvellous baking results. It's great for roasting foil-wrapped corn on the cob, vegetables of all sorts, potatoes, or preparing any "main course" that would heat up your kitchen and make your air conditioner work harder!

6. Indirect "Convection" Cooking

Light just one side of your twin burner and place chicken pieces, ham, turkey, etc. on the grids over the unfired side. This will "bake" the dish without any flare-up. Use this method to bake cakes, pies, breads and cookies, or vegetables . . . any dish into which you don't want an outdoor, smoky flavor imparted.

Steak

Only BROILMASTER® offers up to three different grilling levels that allow you to grill rare, medium and well-done steaks at the same time.

If your BROILMASTER Gas Grill was used for no other purpose than to grill STEAK, it would be worth every cent you paid for it! Steaks grilled outdoors over the "Charmaster" clay briquets of your BROILMASTER still have a flavor unsurpassed by any other cooking method.

Best Choices for Grilling

For best results choose Sirloin, T-Bone, Porterhouse, Filet Mignon (tenderloin), Club, Ribeye. Preferred grades are Prime and Choice.

For great grilling, a steak should be from 1½ to 2 inches thick. 1-inch thickness is minimum. A thin steak quickly becomes overdone and dried out, and loses much of its taste appeal.

Tips For Grilling Steaks

1. Remove steaks from refrigerator 1 to 2 hours before cooking.

2. Trim off excess fat and suet, leaving a thin edge of fat. Score the fat to prevent curling during cooking.

3. Rub salad oil on cooking rack to minimize sticking.

4. Do not salt meat while cooking; salt draws out juices and increases flare-up.

5. Turn steaks with tongs or spatula. Piercing meat with a fork releases juices and increases flare-up.

6. Use higher burner settings and a low grid position for rare steak, and lower burner settings and higher grid position for medium and well-done.

7. To increase smoky flavor, lower lid to one of three positions provided by the lid stop located on the left side of the grill, or close cover completely.

8. Generally, to achieve the most flavorful method, grill steaks with the burner on HI setting and the grill lid closed.

9. Do not leave steaks unattended. For the most delicious and appetizing steaks, be johnny-on-the-spot to turn and remove them from the grill just at the right time!

10. Like that "smoked" taste? For best results use one of the BROILMASTER Grill's Smoker Accessories or sprinkle dampened wood chips on the Charmaster™ clay briquets a few minutes before steaks are done and lower lid. The result — truly smoked flavor!

PORK

Grilled, baked or barbecued on a BROILMASTER® Premium Gas Grill, pork becomes delicious and nutritious food.

Consider these delectable pork possibilities — ¾- to 1-inch thick blade steaks country-style, back ribs, spare ribs, shoulder roast, loin roast, smoked ham, smoked ham slices, kabobs, ground pork, tenderloin, Canadian style bacon, sausage . . . to mention a few cuts. Choose the leaner, meatier cuts of fresh pork and trim off excess fat.

SLOW COOKING BEST

For a real treat, have your butcher cut some 2-inch thick pork loin chops (the leanest and best he has). Grill them on the grids of your BROILMASTER Grill, with the burner at a medium or low setting and the grill lid closed or partially closed. Place grids at a high level.

Season the chops to your liking and turn the chops every 10 or 15 minutes to ensure even cooking. (Use a spatula or tongs . . . not a fork.)

The pork chops should be done in 45 minutes to an hour (if you have resisted the impulse to speed up cooking).

Today's pork is leaner, meatier and more tender. All fresh pork roasts should be cooked to an internal temperature of 170°F for the most juicy, tender and flavorful roast. The meat thermometer should register 160°F for "cook-before-eating" hams, and 40°F for "fully cooked" hams.

Pork roasts vary in shape, size, amount of bone, leanness and thickness. A meat thermometer is the most accurate means of determining doneness. Insert meat thermometer with bulb in thickest part, not touching bone.

When using a Hugga-Rack to prepare a roast, insert meat thermometer at a slight angle so tip is in center of roast but not resting on bone. The thermometer must clear the cooking unit while meat is turning.

HAMBURGERS A LA BROILMASTER®

For flavorful hamburgers use a good grade of beef — ground sirloin, round or chuck.

For extra flavor, mix ground onion with the meat, or add hickory smoke seasoning.

Hamburger patties for grilling should be ½- to ¾-inch thick. Use a HI or MEDIUM burner setting. For a smokier flavor, lower grill lid while cooking.

For rare burgers, use a low grid position. For more well done, use a higher position.

Preheating until the heat indicator reads 400°F or 500°F is suggested, then place burgers on grids and lower lid. Turn once after 4 to 5 minutes.

Second side will need only about half as much cooking time as the first side. Like cheeseburger? Put a slice of Cheddar cheese or Swiss cheese on each patty after it has been turned and close the grill lid for the final minutes.

No time to watch the burger? Place patties in the Hugga-Rack Flat Basket over a medium flame for 10 to 15 minutes.

If you wish to accumulate hamburger patties, use the warming rack. This will hold the hamburger patties far enough away from the flames to prevent over-cooking, but will keep them at serving temperature.

HELPFUL HINTS FOR CERTAIN KINDS OF MEATS, FISH AND FOWL

CHICKEN
HOW TO BROILMASTER® GRILL IT!

Chicken ranks high among America's favorite foods. It can be fried, baked, stewed or grilled. It can be seasoned in limitless ways. Yet, what way of cooking makes this domestic fowl more delicious than grilling over an open fire . . . on a BROILMASTER!

Chickens for surface grilling should be fryers or broilers cut in halves or quarters.

1. SURFACE GRILLED CHICKEN

   a. Preheat grill at medium burner setting for 10 minutes.

   b. Locate cooking grid at top position. Rub surface of grid with cooking oil to minimize sticking.

   c. Place chicken on grid, cavity side down. The lid may be raised or partially lowered. The chicken will cook faster with the lid lowered.

   d. Turn chicken frequently and baste with melted butter, lemon butter or your favorite basting sauce. If chicken is browning too fast, turn burner knob to lower setting. If you wish, you can baste chicken with a barbecue sauce shortly before cooking is completed. Tomato-based and "sweet" barbecue sauces will burn if exposed to the heat too long.

2. ROTISSERIE-GRILLED CHICKEN

   Rotisserie-grilled is a favorite way of barbecuing chicken because it cooks the chicken to an appetizing, even brownness and requires less attention. Chicken may be cooked this way with the grill lid lowered to increase the smoky flavor. Whole chickens may be skewered and clamped and tied into position on the rotisserie spit. The spit will hold two average or three small "broiler" type of chickens. Halves and quarters can easily be grilled in the Hugga-Rack™ Flat Basket.

   Chicken should be brushed occasionally with your favorite basting sauce to keep it moist and tender.

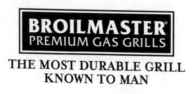

BROILMASTER®
PREMIUM GAS GRILLS

**THE MOST DURABLE GRILL
KNOWN TO MAN**

Spare Ribs

Spare ribs may be completely cooked on the BROILMASTER® Grill using a "LO" flame-setting and grilling with the lid lowered. However, the ribs will be more tender and juicy if partially baked or steamed first . . . then finished on the grill.

Fish

Fish may be baked in heavy foil — adding lemon slices and seasoning before wrapping securely. Fish steaks and fillets, ¾- to 1-inch thick, will require about 10 minutes on each side, cooked with lid lowered (not completely closed) and grill preheated on medium flame. The same method may be used with the Hugga-Rack™ Flat Basket.

Turkeys

With the Hugga-Rack you may grill a turkey up to 20 lbs. in weight, but better results will be obtained with turkeys of 12 to 16 lbs. Never use a pre-basted turkey! It produces too much grease for satisfactory rotisserie grilling and may catch on fire! The turkey can be placed on the Hugga-Grids, stuffed or not, and grilled at low or medium burner setting, with the lid partially lowered. A meat thermometer should be inserted in the breast as a check on doneness.

You may use an indirect method . . . preheat both sides of a twin burner until indicator registers 350-400°F then turn off one half of the burner. Load turkey so it will turn over the unfired side. Preheating this side will help brown the turkey to seal in juices. Cook until meat thermometer registers temperature and finish off by turning on burner under turkey . . . to firm or even "crisp up" the outermost layer.

KABOBS

Kabobs made of cooked meats, cut in 1- to 1½-inch cubes and skewered, may be cooked over medium heat with lid lowered, turning occasionally until heated through. Uncooked pieces of meat cut in 1-inch cubes and marinated overnight can be placed on skewers and cooked over medium heat with lid lowered, turning frequently until done. If vegetables and other foods are to be cooked as kabobs, combine on skewer those foods that will cook in about the same length of time. Also be sure that these foods are about the same size.

WHOLE LOBSTERS

Two small whole lobsters, or from six to eight lobster tails, can be grilled in the Hugga-Rack™ Flat Basket. Brush lobster with melted butter, marinade sauce, or salad oil to keep moist. Cooking time about 20 minutes, or less.

LOBSTER TAILS

Lobster tails can also be surface grilled on the cooking grid with the burner at medium setting. They should be turned frequently to ensure even cooking. Brush with melted butter or salad oil to keep moist. Cooking time, about 15 minutes.

Foil-wrapped lobster can be cooked, with or without stuffing, on the grids with the burner on medium setting and the lid lowered. Cooking time, about 15 minutes.

Keeping Your Broilmaster® Gas Grill in Good Operating Condition

At BROILMASTER, we love to barbecue as much as you do. We know keeping your grill in good working order is important.

The following suggestions do not require a lot of time or effort to take care of your BROILMASTER.

Some users will clean the interior of the grill frequently, using a brass bristle brush and detergent to clean off the deposits of grease and smoke, because they like that "aluminum" look. The majority of users will allow the aluminum surfaces to darken gradually and will concentrate their cleaning efforts on keeping the cooking grids and exterior surfaces of the grill clean, with an occasional washing of the grill interior. A popular method of gas grill hygiene is burning up the grease and food cinders by leaving the burner on "HI" setting and the lid closed for 15 to 20 minutes after cooking is completed. If you use this "no work" method, don't forget to turn off the burner! If the grill is left burning on HI setting for hours (or days), it could damage the finish and castings.

The burners in BROILMASTER Gas Grills are the most rugged and dependable in the gas grill industry. They are constructed of high quality 430 series stainless steel. However, even this rugged and dependable burner should have an occasional cleaning, particularly if the grill is used often or high-fat meats like pork and spare ribs are frequently cooked on it.

Examine the ports that run around the perimeter of the burner. If grease, rust or food cinders are blocking any of the port area, remove them. Be careful not to drop the burner and crack or damage it.

To clean the outside painted surface of your BROILMASTER® Grill, wash occasionally with a mild detergent. The use of the vinyl cover available from your dealer will make the painted finish last longer.

Keep all food preparation surfaces, dishes and utensils clean throughout the entire period of cooking. Use a clean platter for carrying cooked foods from your BROILMASTER Grill.

SOME SELECTED BROILMASTER GAS GRILL RECIPES

Following are a variety of delicious barbecue recipes developed and tested for your enjoyment. You can cook almost anything on your BROILMASTER Grill, so don't limit your outdoor cooking experiences to these recipes. There are many books on barbecuing and outdoor cooking that are rich sources of recipes for foods of all description to cook on your BROILMASTER Gas Grill. Also check with a BROILMASTER® dealer for fine accessories that can help you create "master dishes" outdoors on your grill.

Enjoy!

THE MOST DURABLE GRILL KNOWN TO MAN

APPETIZERS

BROILMASTER®
PREMIUM GAS GRILLS

THE MOST DURABLE GRILL
KNOWN TO MAN

Barbecued Chestnuts

1 lb   chestnuts

With a small, sharp knife, cut a small cross on the side of each chestnut. Place them in a grill basket on the barbecue over moderately high heat and roast the chestnuts, tossing them about from time to time, until the skins are blackened and the flesh inside has softened, about 20 minutes. Yields approximately 2 cups.

Bob's Baby Calamari

Bob buys his baby squid, frozen in packs of 20, from a specialty Chinese grocer.

20   whole, baby calamari, 3 inches long
3 tbsp   Kikoman Teriyaki Marinade Sauce

Toss the calamari with the teriyaki sauce and place on the barbecue over high heat. Cook until the squid turns opaque, about 3 minutes a side. Serves 6.

Cedar-Planked Lobster Cakes with Chili Aioli

1	chipotle chili in adobo sauce
½ cup	mayonnaise
1 tbsp	lemon juice
1½ lbs	cooked lobster meat, torn into ½-inch pieces
2	scallions, finely chopped
1 cup	mayonnaise
2 tbsp	lemon juice
1 cup	bread crumbs
1 tsp	paprika
	salt and pepper

Crush the chipotle chili in a small bowl with the back of a fork. Add the ½ cup mayonnaise and 1 tbsp lemon juice then combine well.

Place the lobster meat in a bowl and add the scallions, 1 cup mayonnaise, 2 tbsp lemon juice, bread crumbs, paprika, salt, and pepper. Combine and form into 8 patties. Choose a plank big enough to accommodate all the lobster cakes. Place the plank, which has been pre-soaked for about 6 hours, on the grill over moderately high heat and heat for about 3 to 5 minutes with the lid of the barbecue down. Place the lobster cakes on the heated cedar plank and cook, with the top down, until they begin to brown a little on top, about 7 minutes. Turn the cakes and continue to cook until done in the center, about another 7 minutes. Serve with chili aioli. Serves 8 as an appetizer.

CHRIS AND ANNE'S SHRIMP WITH MANGO JALAPEÑO SORBET

1 pint	mango sorbet
2	mangos, peeled, pitted, and cut in 1-inch dice
1	jalapeño pepper, seeded and minced
2 tbsp	olive oil
1 tbsp	lime juice
	salt and pepper
12	very large shrimp, peeled with the tails intact

Chill the bowl, lid, and cutting blade of a food processor in the freezer until cold, about 1 hour. Return them to the machine and add the mango sorbet, mangos, and jalapeño pepper. Process until fairly smooth. Remove the cutting blade from the bowl of the processor and return the sorbet to the freezer for about 10 minutes. Form small scoops of the sorbet onto a frozen cookie sheet and return to the freezer.

Combine the olive oil, lime juice, salt, and pepper, then toss the shrimp to coat. Place them on the grill over high heat and cook until they are curled, pink, and opaque throughout. Serve the shrimp on a plate with 2 scoops of the mango jalapeño sorbet. Serves 6 as an hors d'oeuvre.

Cinnamon Pears with Cambazola Cheese

If mache lettuce is unavailable, try baby spinach leaves or a medley of selected greens from mesclin mix.

3	Bosc pears, halved
3 tbsp	canola oil
1 tsp	cinnamon
1 tbsp	maple syrup
1/3	wheel Cambazola cheese, cut into 6 wedges
6	small clusters mache lettuce

Using a melon baller, remove the core from the pears, which have already been cut in half. Put the canola oil in a small dish. Brush the pears with a little of the oil then place them on the barbecue over moderate heat. Grill on three sides until the pears are browned on the outside and tender when pierced with the tip of a knife, about 5 minutes a side. Add the cinnamon and maple syrup to the remaining oil and coat the pears with it for the last few minutes of cooking, basting constantly. Serve on individual plates with the Cambazola cheese wedges and mache lettuce clusters. Serves 6.

Curry Shrimp

1 tbsp	curry powder
1 tbsp	fresh ginger, peeled and grated
3 tbsp	soy sauce
2 tbsp	lime juice
2 tsp	honey
1 lb	large shrimp, peeled with tails intact
4 wedges	lime

Combine the curry powder, ginger, soy sauce, lime juice, and honey in a bowl. Add the shrimp and toss to coat. Marinate for about 30 minutes. Thread the shrimp on two wooden skewers that have been soaked for 30 minutes in water. Space the skewers about ¾ inch apart through each shrimp. This will stabilize the shrimp on the skewers. Place the shrimp skewers on the grill over high heat and cook until pink on the outside and opaque throughout, about 2 to 4 minutes, depending on the size of the shrimp. Serve with lime wedges. Serves 4.

GINGER SHRIMP

1½ lbs	raw shrimp
¼ cup	balsamic vinegar
3 tbsp	soya sauce
¼ cup	olive oil
2 cloves	garlic, peeled and crushed
2 tsp	fresh ginger, peeled and grated
2 tsp	honey
	dash hot pepper sauce

Peel and devein the shrimp, but leave the tails on. Combine the balsamic vinegar, soya sauce, olive oil, garlic, ginger, and honey in a dish, then mix well. Add the shrimp and toss to coat. Marinate 1 hour. Place on the grill in a grill basket, turning as needed, until the shrimp turn pink and are opaque throughout. Serves 6.

Goat Cheese Crostini

1	garlic bud
	olive oil for grilling
	kosher salt
1	4-inch log of goat cheese
3 sprigs	thyme
2	baguettes about 12 inches long
	olive oil for grilling

Cut the garlic bud in half horizontally, so that the root section is one half and the stem section is the other. Brush the surface of the garlic bud halves with olive oil and place cut side down on the barbecue over moderately high heat. Brush the top of the buds with more olive oil and cook until browned. Turn the garlic buds and cook until brown, then adjust so the other half of the uncut side cooks as well. Remove from the grill and set aside until cool enough to handle. Squeeze the garlic cloves from the bud into a small mixing bowl. Sprinkle the garlic with kosher salt and mash until it forms a paste. Cut the log of goat cheese into chunks and mash with the garlic.

Cut the baguettes in half horizontally and then in half vertically, so that there are 8 pieces of bread approximately the same size. Brush the cut surface of the bread with olive oil and place cut side down on a hot grill. Brush the tops of the bread with olive oil and turn when the cut side has browned. When both sides of the bread have browned, remove them to a bread board and spread with the garlic cheese mixture. Serves 8.

JANE AND TERRY'S GRILLED PEPPERS AND GOAT CHEESE

2	green peppers
2	red peppers
1	yellow peppers
½ lb	goat cheese
	freshly ground black pepper
	best quality olive oil
⅓ cup	fresh herbs, such as basil, rosemary, or a mixture of several kinds, finely chopped
	a few sprigs of the same herbs

Blacken the peppers on all sides over high heat. Place in a paper bag to sweat for 10 minutes, then peel the skin. Do not wash. Cut the peppers into strips and set aside. Place the goat cheese in an oiled, fire-proof baking dish, drizzle with olive oil, sprinkle with black pepper and fresh herbs, then heat over medium heat with the barbecue lid down until the cheese is heated through. Crumble the cheese into big lumps in the baking dish and add the peppers. Throw a few herb sprigs on the barbecue coals. Place the dish back on the barbecue, close the lid, and cook until the cheese turns a little golden brown and the peppers are heated through. Serves 6 to 8 as either a starter or side dish.

MUSSELS WITH CHARDONNAY BUTTER

This butter sauce is also good with grilled shrimp.

1 cup	butter
½ cup	onion, peeled and finely chopped
6 cloves	garlic, peeled and minced
½ cup	Chardonnay wine
4 lbs	mussels, scrubbed and debearded

Melt a large spoonful of the butter in a medium saucepan placed on the side burner, over moderate heat. Add the onion and garlic, and cook until softened. Add the Chardonnay and cook until reduced by half. Add the rest of the butter in chunks, incorporating it with a whisk. Remove from heat, but keep warm. Place the mussels in a grill basket on the barbecue over high heat and cook until they open, about 4 to 8 minutes. Discard the ones that don't open. Remove the mussels to a serving platter. Place the butter sauce in a heated bowl and serve with the mussels for dipping. Serves 4.

Mussels with Garlic Almond Butter

½ cup	butter
6 cloves	garlic, mashed
½ cup	blanched almonds, ground
1 cup	white wine
4 lbs	fresh mussels, scrubbed and rinsed

Melt the butter in a small skillet over moderately high heat on the side burner of the barbecue. Add garlic. Cook until softened, but not browned, then add the almonds. Cook until starting to turn golden brown. Add the wine and cook for a few minutes, stirring occasionally.

Meanwhile, place the mussels in a grill basket, set on the barbecue, over high heat. Cook and shift the mussels, as needed, until the shells open. Discard any mussels that don't open. Distribute the mussels among 4 plates and drizzle with the garlic almond butter. Serves 4.

Oysters with Lemon Butter

1 cup	butter
⅓ cup	lemon juice
3 dozen	fresh oysters, scrubbed

Melt the butter on the side burner of the barbecue over moderately high heat. Add the lemon juice. Keep warm on the edge of the barbecue. Place the oysters on the grill over high heat. Cook for about 3 minutes with the lid of the barbecue down. Open the lid and, as the shells open, detach the oysters from the upper shell with an oyster knife. Remove the top shell and discard. Eat them as they come off the grill with a little lemon butter. Serves 6.

Portobello Pizzas

6	3- to 4-inch portobello mushrooms
	olive oil for grilling
¼ cup	pesto sauce
2	tomatoes, cut in ½-inch dice
1 cup	Parmesan Regianno cheese, freshly grated
	olive oil for grilling
	salt and pepper

Remove the stems from the mushrooms by snapping them off. With a small spoon, scrape the dark gills from the underside of the mushroom caps. Brush with olive oil and place on the barbecue, gill side down, over moderately high heat. Cook until the mushrooms are beginning to brown. Brush the tops and turn. Immediately dot the gill side of the mushrooms with pesto sauce, add some tomato and cheese, season with salt and pepper, and drizzle with olive oil. Close the lid of the barbecue and cook until the cheese has melted and the cap side is nicely browned. Serves 6.

Scallops with Caper Butter Sauce

½ cup	butter
¼ cup	capers, drained
2 tbsp	fresh chervil leaves
¼ cup	fresh lemon juice
24	large sea scallops
¼ cup	olive oil
	salt and pepper

Melt the butter in a small saucepan on the side burner of the barbecue over moderate heat. Add the capers, chervil, and lemon juice. Lower the heat and keep warm.

Put the scallops in a bowl, sprinkle with the olive oil, salt and pepper, and toss to coat. Place in a grill basket set on the barbecue over high heat. Cook, turning as needed until browned and barely cooked through. Serve with the caper butter sauce. Serves 6.

SHRIMP WITH WASABI WHIPPED CREAM

Finding Wasabi mustard can be a challenge in remote areas. I found some in a tube that was surprisingly good. Since there is some kind of worldwide shortage of the stuff, it was encouraging to find a good imitation, in a pinch.

1 to 2 tsp	Wasabi mustard
½ cup	whipping cream, whipped
18	large shrimp, peeled, with tails intact
2 tbsp	soy sauce
1 tsp	olive oil
1 tsp	lemon juice
1 tsp	honey
	pickled ginger

Add the mustard in stages to the whipped cream. Stop when it is to your taste.

Combine the soy sauce, olive oil, lemon juice, honey, and ginger. Add the shrimp and toss to coat. Place on the barbecue in a grill basket set over high heat. Cook, turning and brushing when needed, until the shrimp curl and turn pink. Serve with pickled ginger and Wasabi whipped cream. Serves 6.

VAL'S LEGENDARY BAKED BRIE

¼ cup	chopped sun-dried tomatoes
2 tsp	olive oil
2	cloves garlic, minced
1 tbsp	balsamic vinegar
1 tsp	dried basil
⅓ cup	chopped parsley
	pepper
2 125-gram	packages Brie cheese

Cover the tomatoes with boiling water and let stand for 15 minutes. Drain. In a small skillet, heat oil over medium heat. Cook tomatoes, garlic, vinegar, and basil for 1 minute. Remove from heat. Stir in parsley and add pepper to taste. Let cool.

Cut rind off top of each cheese. Place Brie on squares of aluminum foil and top with tomato-parsley mixture. Shape foil loosely up around brie and place on the barbecue over high heat. Close the lid and cook until the cheese softens, about 10 minutes. Serve with baguette slices or crackers. Serves 6 to 8.

BREAD

THE MOST DURABLE GRILL
KNOWN TO MAN

CATHY'S FOCACCIA

Cathy grows fresh herbs beside her barbecue, so that she can add them to dishes when the spirit moves her.

1 tsp	sugar
1 cup	lukewarm water
1	package of yeast
2 tbsp	olive oil
3 cups	flour
1 tsp	salt
	olive oil for grilling
	fresh herbs
	coarse salt

Combine the sugar and water in a small bowl then add the water. Stir briefly and let proof for about 5 minutes. Place the flour and salt in a bowl and combine. Stir the yeast and pour over the flour mixture. Add the olive oil. Stir with a wooden spoon until the dough holds together. Turn the dough out onto a work surface and knead the dough until it is smooth and elastic, about 10 minutes. Place the dough in a large bowl, cover with plastic wrap, and let rise until double in bulk, about 1½ hours. Makes enough dough for 2 focaccias.

Pour some olive oil in a pizza-type pan and roll the dough in it. Prod the dough with your fingertips, expanding it to fit the pan. Alternate with the palm of your hand from time to time. Brush the dough generously with olive oil, then sprinkle with the fresh herbs. Set aside and cover loosely with plastic wrap. Let rise until doubled in bulk. Place on the barbecue over moderate heat and turn the burner off under the focaccia. Cook until the focaccia has browned lightly and the crust is cooked throughout, about 20 to 25 minutes. Sprinkle with the coarse salt. Serves 6.

CATHY'S STICKY BUNS

This is what you make on the barbecue when you cottage on an island without power. Cookies, French bread, bread puddings – Cathy's done it all! For these buns, she uses an enamelled cast-iron baking pan. She has tried all kinds of toppings, but is keen on pecans, dried cherries, dried cranberries, dried blueberries, raisins, and walnuts.

1 cup	milk
½ cup	butter
1 cup	warm water
1 tsp	sugar
2 packages	yeast
2 cups	flour
½ cup	almonds, finely ground
1	apple, peeled, cored, and finely chopped
2	eggs, slightly beaten
1 cup	white sugar
1 tbsp	salt
4 cups	flour
½ cup	butter, melted
1 cup	brown sugar
⅓ cup	maple syrup
½-¾ cup	assorted dried fruit and nuts
¼ cup	melted butter
	brown sugar
	cinnamon

Heat the milk and butter in a small saucepan, until the butter melts. Remove from heat and cool. Place the warm water, sugar, and yeast in a small bowl, cover with a cloth, and allow to sit until the yeast develops, about 5 minutes.

In the bowl of an electric mixer, combine the flour with the butter-milk and yeast mixtures. Run the machine with the dough hook on high speed for about 5 minutes to activate the gluten in the flour. Stir in the almonds, apple, eggs, sugar, and salt.

Turn the dough out onto a work surface and gradually incorporate more flour into the dough, kneading it until it reaches a smooth elastic consistency. Place the dough in a large bowl, cover, and allow to rise until it has doubled in bulk, about 2 hours.

Pour ½ cup butter into a baking pan. Brush it up the sides of the pan, so that the dough will not stick to it. Sprinkle the brown sugar and drizzle the maple syrup over the melted butter. Evenly distribute the dried fruit and/or nuts over the mixture. Set aside.

Punch down the dough and knead again. Roll into a thin rectangle, brush with melted butter, sprinkle thickly with brown sugar and cinnamon, before rolling into a long tube. Slice the tube into 1 inch slices and arrange in the prepared baking pan. Do not pack tightly. Let rise in the pan about 30 minutes. Place the pan on one side of the barbecue over medium-low heat. Close the barbecue lid and turn the burner off under the buns. Cook, turning the pan, so that the side next to the heat source doesn't burn until the buns are cooked through, about 20 to 25 minutes. Place on a rack and allow to cool for a few minutes before turning the buns out of the pan. Serves 8.

Olive and Artichoke Tepanade Pizza

This pizza is also great with homemade pizza dough.

2	medium-size prepared pizza crusts
4 tbsp	tomato sauce
3 tbsp	olive tepanade
2 tbsp	artichoke tepanade
¼ cup	Parmesan cheese, grated
1 tbsp	olive oil

Spread the prepared pizza crusts with the tomato sauce. Dot the top with olive and artichoke tepanade. Sprinkle the pizzas with the Parmesan cheese and then drizzle with the olive oil. Slide the pizzas onto one side of the grill over moderately high heat and turn the burner off under the pizza. Close the lid and cook until the cheese on the top of the pizza begins to bubble, about 4 to 5 minutes. Serves 2.

Tomato Mushroom and Black Olive Pizza

1 tbsp	olive oil
1	small onion, peeled and finely chopped
1 clove	garlic, peeled and minced
4	plum tomatoes, peeled and chopped
1 tbsp	fresh basil, finely chopped
	salt and pepper
½ recipe	pizza dough
	olive oil for grilling
6	mushrooms, cleaned and thinly sliced
1 dozen	black olives, pitted and cut in several pieces
½ cup	freshly grated Parmigiano Reggiano cheese

Heat the olive oil in a medium saucepan over moderately high heat on the side burner of the barbecue. Add the onion and cook until softened, about 4 minutes. Add the garlic and cook for another minute or so. Do not brown the onion and garlic. Add the chopped tomatoes and basil, then season with salt and pepper. Cook until the sauce thickens, about 5 minutes, and set aside.

Using half of one recipe of pizza dough, prod the dough with your fingertips all over to form a circle about 1 inch thick. With a rolling pin, roll the circle of dough in several directions until the dough is uniformly about ¼ inch thick. Place the circle of dough on a cookie sheet then slide it onto the grill over moderate heat. Close the lid and cook for about 2 minutes. Check the underside of the pizza and turn when there are brown grid marks seared onto the bottom of the dough and some browning of the crust has started, about 2 to 3 minutes. Brush the cooked side with olive oil and immediately add the tomato sauce, mushrooms, olives, and grated cheese. Close the lid on the barbecue and cook until the cheese has melted, about 3 or 4 minutes. Cut into 8 wedges and serve. Serves 4 as a starter and 1 or 2 as a main course, depending on the level of your hunger.

PIZZA DOUGH

1 package	yeast
1 tbsp	sugar
1 cup	lukewarm water
3 cups	flour
1 tsp	salt

Combine the sugar and water in a small warm bowl. Add the yeast and stir briefly. Let proof for about 5 minutes. Place the flour and salt in a bowl and combine. Stir the yeast and pour over the flour mixture. Stir with a wooden spoon until the dough holds together. Place on a work surface and knead until the dough is smooth and elastic, about 10 minutes. Put the dough in a medium-size bowl, cover with plastic wrap, and let rise until doubled in bulk, about 1½ hours. Knead the dough again for about 2 minutes, divide into 2 portions, and form into pizza crusts. Unused dough can be frozen for later use. Let dough return to room temperature before handling.

Desserts

THE MOST DURABLE GRILL
KNOWN TO MAN

Apples with Cinnamon-Caramel Sauce

1½ cups	brown sugar
½ cup	water
1 tbsp	lemon juice
1 stick	cinnamon, 4 inches in length, split
1 piece	lemon rind, 1 inch wide and 2 inches long
3	Golden Delicious apples
½ cup	canola oil
1 tsp	ground cinnamon
1 tbsp	lemon juice
	vanilla ice cream

Place the brown sugar, water, lemon juice, cinnamon stick, and lemon peel in a medium saucepan over high heat on the side burner of the barbecue and bring to a boil, stirring constantly. Reduce the heat to low and simmer until the liquid becomes syrupy. Strain and keep warm.

Cut the apples in half, trim away the stems, and remove the cores with a melon baller. Cut the halves in half. Combine the canola oil, cinnamon, and lemon juice in a dish then add the apples. Toss to coat. Place the apples in a grill basket on the barbecue over moderately high heat and cook, basting and turning as needed until the apples are browned on the outside and tender when pierced with the tip of a knife. Serve with the cinnamon-caramel sauce over vanilla ice cream. Serves 4.

Chocolate Marshmallow Sundae

	chocolate ice cream
2 tbsp	strong coffee
2 tbsp	corn syrup
3 tbsp	butter
4 oz	semi-sweet chocolate, cut into small chunks
6	white marshmallows
6	chocolate marshmallows

Put 6 glass compotes into the freezer and chill for at least 1 hour. About 1 hour before serving, put 2 scoops of the ice cream into each of the compotes and return to the freezer.

Meanwhile, on the side burner of the barbecue in a small saucepan, heat the coffee, corn syrup, and butter over high heat until it comes to a boil. Boil for 30 seconds and remove from the heat. Let stand for 30 seconds and then add the chocolate. Stir until smooth. Keep warm until ready to use.

Thread the marshmallows onto skewers. Place on the barbecue over high heat and cook until they are soft throughout. Remove the compotes of ice cream from the freezer and add the chocolate sauce. Slide the marshmallows off the skewers directly onto the sundaes. Top each one with one vanilla and one chocolate marshmallow. Serves 6.

Clare's Peaches with Butterscotch Sauce

6	peaches, peeled, cut in half, and pits removed
2 tbsp	ground almonds
1	small piece of angelica cut into 12 slivers (optional)
½ cup	butter
1½ cups	brown sugar
1 cup	whipping cream

Place the peach halves cut side up on a piece of barbecue-strength foil. Put 1 tsp of ground almonds and a sliver of angelica in each peach half. Wrap them in foil making a package and place on the barbecue over moderate heat. Cook until tender, about 20 minutes.

In a medium saucepan over moderate heat, melt the butter. Stir in the brown sugar and add the cream. Cook, stirring occasionally until the mixture thickens, about 10 to 12 minutes. Serve with the peaches. Serves 6.

Glazed Lemon Loaf with Berries and Whipped Cream

1 cup	butter
1 cup	sugar
3	eggs
1½ cups	flour
1 tsp	baking powder
¼ tsp	salt
½ cup	milk
2 tbsp	large grated lemon peel
½ pint	whipping cream, whipped
½ tsp	vanilla
1 tbsp	icing sugar
¼ cup	fresh lemon juice
½ cup	sugar
1 pint	fresh raspberries

Cream the butter and sugar, then add the eggs. Combine the flour, baking powder, and salt, and mix well. Add the flour mixture to the butter mixture, alternately with the milk. Stir in the lemon peel and pour the batter into a loaf pan. Bake in a 350°F oven until a cake tester or broom strand comes out clean when inserted in the center of the loaf. Cool.

Add the vanilla and icing sugar to the whipped cream, then set aside. Keep chilled.

Combine the icing sugar and lemon juice. Cut 8 1-inch slices from the loaf and place on the grill over high heat. Cook until lightly toasted and warm inside, about 2 minutes a side. Brush the lemon juice mixture thickly on the loaf slices while they are still hot from the grill. Serve with the raspberries and a dollop of whipped cream. Serves 8.

Howard's Bananas

Howard likes an orange flavor with his bananas, but he says Tia Maria imparts a wonderful coffee flavor and is very popular with his guests. In any case, he likes to drench the banana with it, so the measurement below may be stingy. Howard is big on those spray bottles of whipped cream, but I have included the ingredients for homemade whipped cream for those who prefer it.

4	bananas
½ cup	Grand Marnier
¾ cup	whipping cream, whipped
½ tsp	vanilla
1 tbsp	icing sugar

Place the bananas on the grill over high heat and cook until they are brown all over and sweating. Unzip the banana with the cut of a sharp knife and remove the whole fruit. Place each banana on a dessert plate and spoon 2 tbsp of Grand Marnier or the liqueur of choice over top. Combine the whipped cream with the vanilla and icing sugar. Place in a pastry bag and pipe along the length of the banana or add a dollop on the side. Serves 4.

Maple-Balsamic Strawberries with Grilled Pound Cake

3 tbsp	maple syrup
2 tsp	balsamic vinegar
18 large	strawberries with leaves attached
1 pound	cake, sliced 1-inch thick
¼ cup	butter, softened
1 cup	whipping cream, whipped and sweetened with maple syrup

Combine the maple syrup and balsamic vinegar in a small bowl. Thread 6 strawberries on each of three wooden skewers. Brush each of the skewers with the maple mixture. Place them on the barbecue over high heat and cook about 3 minutes a side on 4 sides, brushing with the marinade half way through, until the strawberries are grilled on all sides. Remove from skewers.

Meanwhile, spread one side of each slice of pound cake with butter and place on the grill over high heat, buttered side down. Immediately spread the other side with butter. Cook until lightly toasted, turn and cook the other side. Place on individual plates along with a dollop of sweetened whipped cream and 3 strawberries. Serves 6.

Pineapple with Citrus Cardamom Caramel Sauce

	seeds from 24 green cardamom pods
½ cup	orange juice
¼ cup	lemon juice
1 cup	brown sugar
1 tbsp	butter
1½ cups	heavy cream, whipped
1 tsp	vanilla
1 tbsp	icing sugar
2	pineapples
2 tbsp	canola oil
1 tsp	cardamom, ground

Crush the cardamom seeds so that they release a little fragrance. Place them and the orange juice, lemon juice, brown sugar, and butter in a medium saucepan on the side burner of the barbecue over moderately high heat. When the liquid comes to a boil, reduce the heat to low and simmer until the mixture becomes syrupy. Strain and return to the saucepan to keep warm.

Add the vanilla and icing sugar to the whipped cream and reserve. Cut the stem end from the pineapples and trim the skin and eyes from the sides and bottom. Cut the pineapples into 8 wedges. Trim the tough core from each wedge. Combine the canola oil and cardamom, then brush mixture on the pineapple wedges. Place on the barbecue over moderately high heat and cook, turning as needed and brushing with the oil mixture until the pineapple is browned on the outside and heated through. Serve in a pool of the sauce with a dollop of whipped cream. Serves 4.

Drinks

Andrea's Chocolate Martini

Andrea uses the coffee bean for a mocha flavor, otherwise she opts for the chocolate curl, made by running a small paring knife along the edge of a warm chunk of chocolate.

2 oz	vodka
1 oz	crème de cacao
2	ice cubes
	coffee bean or chocolate curl for garnish

Combine the vodka, crème de cacao, and ice in a shaker. Shake and pour into a martini glass without the ice cubes. Garnish with a coffee bean. Serves 1.

Brad's Fig Martini

2 oz	vodka
1 oz	Feigling liqueur
2	ice cubes

Combine the vodka, liqueur, and ice in a shaker. Shake and pour into a martini glass without the ice cubes. Serves 1.

Bruce's Urban Destroyer

4	large ice cubes
1¼ oz	dark rum
5 oz	Seaman's old-fashioned orange drink
	juice from ½ lime, spent lime reserved

Place ice cubes in a tall glass. Add rum, orange drink, and lime juice to the glass and stir. Garnish with spent lime shell. Serves 1.

Carey's White Wine Sangria

2	limes
1	orange
1	lemon
1	nectarine or peach
½ cup	sugar
½ cup	orange liqueur
½ cup	brandy
2 750-ml	bottles dry white wine
1 750-ml	bottle soda water
	ice cubes

Cut the fruit into wedges or slices and place in a very large pitcher. Add the sugar, liqueur, brandy, and wine, then stir well. Cover and refrigerate for approximately 4 hours. Just before serving, add lots of ice and the soda water to the pitcher. Serves 12.

Green Iced Tea

2	dozen ice cubes
1	pot of brewed green tea, cooled to room temperature
1 tbsp	honey
4 slices	unpeeled fresh ginger
4 wedges	lime

Place the ice in 4 tall glasses. Add the honey to the tea pot and stir until dissolved. Pour the tea over the ice then add the ginger and lime. Serves 4.

Mint Lemonade

¼ cup	mint leaves, cut fresh from the stems
1 cup	boiling water
1 12-oz can	frozen, concentrated lemonade
2 cans	water
6 sprigs	fresh mint
1	lemon cut in ¼-inch thick slices

Place the mint leaves in a bowl and add boiling water. Let stand for 5 minutes. Strain the liquid into a pitcher and discard the mint leaves. Add the lemonade and water, and stir well. Add ice, fresh mint sprigs, and lemon slices. Serves 6.

The Stewart Manhattan

6 oz	rye whisky
2 oz	dry vermouth
¼ oz	Angostura bitters
4 dashes	orange bitters *or*
4 drops	pure orange extract

Pour ingredients over ice in a pitcher. Stir to chill. Serve in chilled martini glasses. Garnish with a maraschino cherry. Serves 4.

Strawberry–Lemon Slush

2 cups	fresh strawberries, stems removed
1 cup	sugar
3 cups	water, divided
1 cup	fresh lemon juice
	crushed ice
4	large strawberries with the stems intact, for garnish
4 wedges	lemon, for garnish

Purée the strawberries in a blender. Combine the sugar, 1 cup of water and the lemon juice. Stir until the sugar has dissolved. Add the other 2 cups of water and the puréed strawberries. Combine well. Pour into glasses containing the crushed ice and add a whole strawberry and a lemon wedge for garnish. Serves 4.

FISH

THE MOST DURABLE GRILL
KNOWN TO MAN

Arctic Char with Melon Relish

½ cup	cantaloupe, skinned, seeded, and cut in ½-inch dice
½ cup	honeydew melon, skinned, seeded, and cut in ½-inch dice
½ cup	yellow watermelon, rinds removed, seeded, and cut in ½-inch dice
¼ cup	red onion, peeled and finely chopped
2 tbsp	golden raisins
¼ cup	pine nuts, lightly toasted
2 tbsp	fresh mint leaves, finely cut
1½ tbsp	olive oil
2 tbsp	champagne vinegar
	salt and pepper
2	whole Arctic char, about 1 lb each
2 tbsp	olive oil
1 tbsp	lemon juice
1 tbsp	fresh thyme leaves
	salt and pepper

Combine the cantaloupe, honeydew melon, and watermelon in a bowl. Add the onion, raisins, pine nuts, mint, olive oil, vinegar, salt, and pepper. Toss to coat. Set aside.

Combine the 2 tbsp olive oil, lemon juice and thyme, then brush on the steaks. Season with salt and pepper before placing on the barbecue over high heat. Cook until the outside is browned and the fish is opaque throughout, about 8 minutes a side, depending on the thickness of fish. Serve the fish cut in individual portions with the melon relish. Serves 6.

Blackened Salmon

1 tbsp	Hungarian paprika
1½ tsp	cayenne
2 tsp	garlic powder
1 tsp	dried ground thyme
2 tsp	salt
2 tsp	pepper
½ cup	butter, melted
1 4-lb	salmon filet

Combine the paprika, cayenne, garlic powder, thyme, salt, and pepper. Place the filet on a platter, brush with the melted butter, and sprinkle with the spice mixture. Place the filet, flesh side down on the barbecue, over moderately high heat. Cook until the flesh side is nicely browned, about 5 minutes. Brush the skin-side with the butter, turn the salmon, and cook until the skin-side of the salmon is browned and the salmon is just opaque throughout, about another 5 to 8 minutes. Serves 6.

Cedar-Planked Salmon with Basil

Make sure that you cut your planks to the right length to accommodate your salmon, while not forgetting to consider the size of your barbecue as well. Soak the planks about 6 hours.

1 side	Atlantic Salmon filet, about 2½ or 3 lbs
	coarse salt
2	lemons, thinly sliced
1	lime, thinly sliced
1 large bunch	fresh basil
1	red onion, peeled and thickly sliced
	salt and pepper

Check your salmon to ensure that all the pin bones are removed. Brush both sides of the salmon with olive oil. Place the plank on the barbecue over high heat and cook for about 4 or 5 minutes until the plank begins to make a crackling noise. Sprinkle the plank generously with the coarse salt. Spread the plank with a layer of lemon and lime slices approximately where the fish will lie. Distribute a few stems of basil on top of the lemons. Place the salmon on the bed of lemons, limes, and basil. Layer lemons, limes, basil, and onions on top of the salmon and season with salt and pepper. Cook until the salmon is just cooked through, about 15 minutes or so. Be prepared to douse any flames from the plank with water. Serves 6.

Halibut with Beurre Noir

4	halibut steaks
	olive oil for grilling
½ cup	butter
6 tbsp	fresh lemon juice
3 tbsp	capers
1 tbsp	fresh parsley, minced
	salt and pepper

Brush the steaks with oil then sprinkle with salt and pepper. Place over hot coals and cook about 4 minutes a side until barely cooked through. Meanwhile, in a medium skillet over moderate heat on the side burner, melt the butter until it turns a nut-brown color. Remove from heat and add the lemon juice. Stir to halt the browning of the butter. Stir in the capers, parsley, and seasoning. Pour the sauce over the halibut. Serves 4.

Halibut with Sun-Dried Tomatoes and Olives

The tomato-olive salsa is a very rich accompaniment. I suggest a light green salad on the side with a simple dressing of olive oil and lemon juice.

6	halibut steaks
	olive oil for grilling
	salt and pepper
1	small red onion, peeled and chopped
4 cloves	garlic, peeled and crushed
½ cup	olive oil
3 tbsp	balsamic vinegar
¼ cup	oil-packed, sun-dried tomatoes, drained and coarsely chopped
1 cup	black olives, pitted and coarsely chopped

Place the olive oil in a small skillet on the side burner over medium heat and add the onion. Cook, stirring occasionally, until the onion is soft. Add the garlic and cook two more minutes. Remove the pan from the heat and pour the contents into a medium-sized serving bowl. Add the vinegar, tomatoes, and olives. Season with salt and pepper. Keep at room temperature while grilling the fish. Brush one side of the fish with the oil, then season with salt and pepper. Place the fish oiled-side down on a hot grill and cook for about 4 minutes. Brush the top of the fish with more olive oil, then season it. Turn the fish and grill another few minutes until just cooked through. Serve with the tomato-olive mixture. Serves 6.

J & S Shrimp Kebabs on Saffron Basmati Rice

1 tbsp	olive oil
2 tbsp	onion, peeled and minced
¼ tsp	saffron threads
1 cup	basmati rice
2	cups water
¼ tsp	salt
2	red onions, peeled
24	jumbo shrimp, peeled and deveined with tails intact
16	cherry tomatoes
1	bunch asparagus, cut into 1½-inch pieces
1	bottle of mango chutney
	olive oil for the grill
1 tbsp	olive oil
2 tbsp	onion, peeled and minced
¼ tsp	saffron threads
1 cup	basmati rice

Heat the olive oil in a medium saucepan set on the side burner of the barbecue over moderate heat. Add the onion and cook until softened. Add the saffron and rice, then stir for about 30 seconds. Add the water and salt, then bring the mixture to a boil, stirring occasionally. Cover the pot, reduce the heat to low, and simmer until the rice is done, about 20 to 25 minutes.

Cut the onions in half, then each half in quarters. Thread the onions, shrimp, tomatoes, and asparagus onto 8 kebabs, alternating the ingredients. Put the mango chutney in a bowl and stir until smooth. Brush the grill lightly with the olive oil and let the excess burn off. Brush the kebabs with the chutney and place on the grill over moderate heat. Cook, turning and basting as needed, until the shrimp are opaque throughout, about 10 minutes. Serve on a large spoonful of the saffron basmati rice. Serves 4.

Robert's Seafood Pasta

My son, Robert, had enjoyed this dish in a restaurant and described it to me. I did what he thought I should do to make it and the result was fantastic.

1 dozen	large shrimp
1 dozen	sea scallops
4	baby squid
	olive oil for grilling
	salt and pepper
½ lb	littleneck clams
½ lb	mussels
1 450-gm	package of spaghetti
¼ cup	olive oil
6 cloves	garlic, peeled and minced
2	tomatoes, cut in ½-inch dice
1 tbsp	fresh basil leaves, minced
	salt and pepper
	Parmesan cheese

Bring a large pot of water to a boil over high heat.

Arrange the seafood on a platter. Brush the shrimp, scallops, and squid with olive oil, and season with salt and pepper. Place the shrimp and scallops in a grill basket and set on the barbecue over high heat. Place the baby squid directly on the grill. Cook until browned on the outside and opaque throughout. Place on a clean platter for serving. When the shrimp and scallops are finished, put the clams and mussels in the grill basket and cook until they open. Discard any that do not.

Meanwhile, after you start grilling the clams and mussels, add the pasta to the boiling water. Cook, stirring occasionally, until al dente — tender but firm — about 10 to 11 minutes.

Meanwhile, on the side burner of the barbecue, heat the ¼ cup of olive oil in a large skillet over moderate heat. Add the garlic and cook about 30 seconds. Add the tomatoes, basil, and grilled seafood, then stir until heated through. Season with salt and pepper. Serve with the pasta and top if desired with Parmesan cheese. Serves 4.

Salmon Steaks with Corn Spoon Bread

4 ears	corn, husks removed
	olive oil for grilling
	salt and pepper
2 tbsp	olive oil
½ cup	onion, peeled and finely chopped
3 cups	milk
¾ cup	cornmeal
1½ cups	old cheddar cheese, grated
2 tbsp	thyme leaves, minced
	salt and pepper
5	eggs, separated
	butter for greasing pan
6	salmon steaks
3 tbsp	olive oil
½ tsp	cayenne pepper
	salt and pepper

Brush the ears of corn with olive oil then season with salt and pepper. Place the corn on the barbecue over moderately high heat and cook, turning as needed, until the corn is tender, about 7 to 10 minutes. Cut the corn kernels from the cob and set aside.

Melt the 2 tbsp olive oil in a medium saucepan on the side burner of the barbecue over moderate heat. Add the onions and cook until softened, about 3 minutes. Add the milk and heat for a minute. Add the cornmeal and combine well with a whisk. Using a wooden spoon, stir and cook the cornmeal until the mixture thickens, about 10 minutes. Remove from the heat and stir in the corn, cheese, and thyme. Bring the mixture to room temperature. Season with salt and pepper. Add the egg yolks, one at a time. Beat the egg whites until they hold stiff peaks. Fold a spoonful of the whites into the cornmeal mixture and combine. Fold in the rest. Butter a stainless steel or enamelled cast-iron baking dish and add the corn spoon bread batter.

Place a roasting pan on one side of the barbecue over moderately low heat. Place the pudding baking dish into the roasting pan and add enough boiling water to measure half way up the side of the baking dish. Lower the lid of the barbecue and cook until the bread is puffed and golden brown, about 30 minutes. Set aside and keep warm.

Combine the olive oil and cayenne, then coat the salmon steaks with the mixture. Season them with salt and pepper. Place the steaks on the barbecue over high heat and cook until the salmon is opaque throughout, about 4 minutes on each side. Serve with the corn spoon bread. Serves 6.

Salmon Steaks with Cucumber Salsa

1	cucumber, peeled, seeded, and cut in ¼-inch dice
1 tbsp	fresh chives, finely chopped
1 tbsp	fresh dill, finely chopped
1 tbsp	fresh parsley, finely chopped
	juice of 1 lime
2 tbsp	white balsamic vinegar
2 tsp	olive oil
	salt and pepper
4	salmon steaks
	olive oil for grilling
	salt and pepper

Combine the cucumber, herbs, lime juice, vinegar, olive oil, salt, and pepper. Mix well and set aside.

Brush the salmon steaks with olive oil, sprinkle with salt and pepper, and place on the grill over high heat. Cook until the salmon is browned on both sides and just opaque on the inside. Serve with the cucumber salsa. Serves 4.

Salmon with Tomato Corn Ragout

1 3-lb	filet of salmon, with skin on
	olive oil for grilling
¼ cup	olive oil
1 tbsp	fresh mint, chopped
	salt and pepper
1 tbsp	olive oil
1 tbsp	butter
1	red onion, peeled and chopped
2 cups	fresh corn kernels
1	jalapeño pepper, seeded and minced
2	tomatoes, seeded and chopped
3 tbsp	fresh mint, chopped
	salt and pepper

Place the salmon skin side up on a work surface and brush with a little olive oil. Combine the ¼ cup olive oil, mint, salt, and pepper. Turn the fish skin side down and brush with the olive oil mixture. Place the salmon on the grill over moderately high heat and close the lid of the barbecue. Cook about 10 minutes and then start to check for doneness. The flesh should start to flake on the thinnest areas of the fish when it is done.

Meanwhile, melt the olive oil and butter in a medium skillet over moderate heat on the side burner of the barbecue. Add the onions and cook until softened. Add the corn and the jalapeño pepper and cook until the corn is tender, about 3 minutes. Stir in the tomatoes and cook until they are heated through, about another 3 minutes. Add the mint and season with salt and pepper. Serve with the salmon. Serves 6.

Shark Skewers with Mango and Cherry Tomatoes

1 1-lb	shark steak
2 tbsp	olive oil
1 tbsp	white balsamic vinegar
1 tbsp	lime juice
1 tbsp	fresh mint, minced
	salt and pepper
1	barely ripe mango, pitted, peeled, and cut in 1-inch dice
1 pint	red and yellow cherry tomatoes
2	limes, cut into slices

Cut the shark into 1-inch chunks. Combine the olive oil, vinegar, lime juice, mint, salt, and pepper in a bowl, and add the shark. Marinate for about 15 minutes, but no longer, as the vinegar and lime will "cook" the fish.

Thread the shark, mango, tomatoes, and lime slices alternately on 6 skewers which have been soaked in water for an hour or more and place on the grill over high heat. Cook, turning frequently and basting with the fish marinade, until the fish is opaque throughout and browned, about 4 to 6 minutes. Serves 6.

Slemon Whisky Salmon

The Slemons say that you should not change the amount of salt and pepper. It is "right on."

1 whole	Pacific salmon
1 tbsp	brown sugar
1 tbsp	molasses
½ cup	whisky
½ cup	olive oil
2 tbsp	soy sauce
2 cloves	garlic, peeled and minced
1 tbsp	salt
1 tbsp	pepper

Remove the head, tail, and fins from the salmon. Run a sharp knife down the backbone of the fish until it opens flat. Place the fish flesh side down in a large dish. Remove the backbone.

Combine the brown sugar, molasses, whisky, olive oil, soy sauce, garlic, salt, and pepper. Pour the mixture over the salmon and marinate overnight in the refrigerator. Remove salmon from the marinade and place it skin side down on a piece of barbecue-strength foil. Place the foil with the fish on the grill over moderately high heat and cook until the fish just begins to flake and the centre is just opaque, about 20 to 30 minutes. Serves 6 to 8 people depending on the size of the fish.

STRIPED SEA BASS WITH ROASTED RED PEPPER AND TOMATO SAUCE

4	red peppers
2	fresh plum tomatoes
8 cloves	garlic, peeled and minced
2	shallots, peeled and finely chopped
¼ tsp	cayenne pepper
½ tsp	hot sauce
½ cup	olive oil
	salt and pepper
1 2-lb	whole sea bass, scaled, fins removed
	olive oil for grilling
	salt and pepper

Place the whole peppers on the barbecue over high heat and cook, turning as needed, until charred on all sides. Place in a paper bag for 5 minutes to sweat. Rub the skins off the peppers, cut them in half, remove the seeds, and cut into slices. Cut the tomatoes in half and place on the barbecue over moderately high heat. Cook until heated through. Cool. Place the tomatoes, pepper slices, garlic, shallots, cayenne, hot sauce, and olive oil in the bowl of a food processor and process until smooth. Season with salt and pepper, then place in a small saucepan to warm on the side burner of the barbecue.

Brush the striped sea bass with olive oil and season with salt and pepper. Place the fish on the barbecue over moderately high heat and cook until browned on both sides and just opaque on the inside, about 10 to 15 minutes, depending on the thickness of the fish. Cut serving-size portions from the fish, removing the skin and bones where possible, and place on a pool of sauce on each plate. Serves 4.

Swordfish Steak with Roasted Pepper Pesto

3	red bell peppers
1	jalapeño pepper
3 cloves	garlic, peeled and cut in half
¼ cup	fresh basil leaves
2 tbsp	olive oil
2 tsp	balsamic vinegar
	salt and freshly ground pepper
½ cup	olive oil
½ tsp	cayenne pepper
½ tsp	hot sauce
2 lbs	swordfish steak, cut 1¼ inches thick
4 wedges	lemon

Roast the peppers over very hot coals until the outer skin is blackened all over. Place the peppers in a paper bag for 5 or 10 minutes to sweat. Remove and peel away the outer skin. Cut the peppers open to remove the seeds and inner membranes. Place the peppers in the bowl of a food processor with the garlic, basil, olive oil, and vinegar. Process until almost smooth.

Combine the ½ cup of olive oil, cayenne pepper, and hot sauce, then pour over the steak. Place the swordfish on the barbecue over high heat and cook, brushing with the oil and turning as needed until the outside is browned, but the inside is just barely pink. Serve with the pesto and lemon wedges. Serves 4.

TERIYAKI SALMON

¼ cup   soya sauce
1 tbsp   olive oil
2 cloves   garlic, crushed
1 tsp   fresh ginger, grated
1 tsp   demerara sugar
4   salmon steaks
4 wedges   lemon

Combine the soya sauce, olive oil, garlic, ginger, and sugar in a dish, then add the salmon. Marinate 45 to 60 minutes. Grill over high heat, brushing with the marinade and turning once, until the steaks are nicely browned and opaque throughout. Garnish with lemon wedges. Serves 4.

TROUT FILETS WITH MANGO PEACH SALSA

½	mango, pitted, cut into ½ inch sections, and then cut from the peel
2	peaches, peeled, stoned and cut in ½ inch dice
1 tsp	maple syrup
1 tbsp	lemon juice
1 tbsp	white balsamic vinegar
1 tbsp	fresh mint leaves, finely chopped
3	pink trout filets with skin still attached, about 3 lbs
	olive oil
	salt and pepper

Combine the mango, peaches, maple syrup, lemon juice, balsamic vinegar, and mint, then mix well. Set aside and chill.

Brush both sides of the trout with olive oil and sprinkle the flesh side with salt and pepper. Place on the grill over moderately high heat and cook without turning until the fish is opaque throughout, about 10 minutes. Serve the trout in portions, removed from the skin and topped with a spoonful of salsa. Serves 6 to 8.

Meat

THE MOST DURABLE GRILL
KNOWN TO MAN

Back Ribs with Sambal Barbecue Sauce

1 cup	chili sauce
1 tbsp	Sambal Oelek (Vietnamese chili paste)
3 sticks	cinnamon, 3 inches long
1 tbsp	fresh ginger, peeled and grated
1 tbsp	coarsely grated lemon peel
¼ cup	lemon juice
1 tbsp	honey
2 full racks	pork back spareribs, about 4 lbs
	salt and pepper

Combine chili sauce, Sambal Oelek, cinnamon, ginger, lemon peel, lemon juice, and honey in a medium saucepan. Place over moderately low heat, bring to a boil, and cook for about 15 minutes.

Meanwhile, sprinkle the racks of spareribs with salt and pepper. Place in a roasting pan and cover with foil. Place the pan in a 450°F oven and cook until no longer pink, about 15 minutes. Remove the ribs from the roasting pan and place on the grill over moderate coals. After 5 minutes, turn and brush with a thick coating of sauce. Cook about 5 minutes and turn again. Brush the remaining side with another thick coating of sauce and grill until browned. Serves 6.

Beef Ribs with Tangy Barbecue Sauce

1½ tbsp	olive oil
6 cloves	garlic, peeled and minced
1	onion, peeled and chopped
1	jalapeño pepper, seeded and minced
5 tbsp	brown sugar
3 tbsp	molasses
1½ cups	ketchup
⅓ cup	malt vinegar
¼ cup	brewed coffee
¼ cup	beer
1 tbsp	Dijon mustard
1 tbsp	Worcestershire sauce
	salt and pepper
3 lbs	beef ribs

Put oil in a skillet and place on the side burner of the barbecue over moderate heat. Add the onion, garlic, and jalapeño pepper. Cook until tender, about 5 minutes, then add the other ingredients. Return the mixture to a simmer, reduce the heat to low, and cook until thickened, stirring occasionally, for about 20 minutes.

Meanwhile, bring a large pot of water to a boil over high heat and add the ribs. Reduce the heat to moderately low and cook until the ribs are just cooked through, about 10 to 20 minutes. Remove the ribs and brush with the barbecue sauce. Place on the barbecue over moderate heat and cook until the sauce becomes a nice glaze, about 5 minutes a side. Serves 6.

Chili Steak

½ cup	mayonnaise
4-8	chipotle chilies in adobo sauce
	salt and pepper
6	filets mignon cut about 1-inch thick

Mash the chipotle chilies in a bowl and add the mayonnaise, salt, and pepper. Coat the steaks with the mixture and place on the grill over high heat. Cook about 4 to 6 minutes a side until cooked to desired doneness. Let rest for a few minutes and serve. Serves 6.

Demerara Sugar Ribs

⅓ cup	demerara sugar
⅔ cup	soy sauce
¼ cup	hoisin sauce
2 tbsp	dry sherry
2 tbsp	fresh ginger, peeled and grated
5 cloves	garlic, peeled and minced
	salt and pepper
4 lbs	pork spareribs, cut into 4 equal portions

Combine the sugar, soy sauce, hoisin sauce, sherry, ginger, garlic, salt, and pepper in a small bowl and mix well. Place the ribs on a platter and coat with the marinade. Refrigerate for about 4 hours. Remove the ribs from the marinade and let it drip off the ribs. Reserve the marinade. Place the ribs on the barbecue over moderately high heat and turn and cook until the ribs have browned all over. Brush the reserved marinade on the ribs and continue to brush, turn, and cook until the ribs run clear when pierced with a skewer at the thickest point. Serves 4.

Filets Mignon with Pinot Noir Sauce

3 tbsp	olive oil
4	shallots, peeled and minced
5 sprigs	fresh parsley
3 sprigs	fresh thyme
3 cups	Pinot Noir wine
2 cups	beef stock
	salt and pepper
6	filets mignon, wrapped with bacon
6 sprigs	fresh thyme, for garnish

Heat the oil in a large saucepan set over moderate heat on the side burner of the barbecue. Add the shallots and fresh herbs, and cook until the shallots have turned a golden brown. Add the Pinot Noir and raise the temperature to high. Boil the sauce until it is reduced to about ½ cup. Add the beef stock and boil again to about ¾ cup. Season with salt and pepper, then strain the sauce through a fine sieve. Keep warm until beef is done.

Meanwhile, place the steaks on the barbecue over high heat and cook 3 to 5 minutes a side until browned on the outside, but still pink on the inside. Let stand for about 5 minutes. Serve in a pool of sauce with a few sprigs of fresh thyme on top. Serves 6.

FRUIT-STUFFED PORK TENDERLOIN WITH PORT SAUCE

1 tbsp	olive oil
2 cloves	garlic, peeled and minced
1 cup	port
1 tbsp	butter
1 tsp	honey
1 large	pork tenderloin
10	dried apricots
¼ cup	dried cranberries
¼ cup	dried pineapple
¼ cup	golden raisins
¼ cup	chèvre cheese
2 tbsp	olive oil
2 tbsp	fresh sage leaves, minced
	salt and pepper

Heat the olive oil in a medium skillet over moderate heat and add the garlic. Add the port and raise the heat to high. Cook until the port sauce is reduced to about ¼ cup. Add the butter and honey then continue to cook for another minute or two. Set the sauce aside and either keep warm or quickly reheat before serving.

Make a cut along the length of the tenderloin that makes it possible to lay the tenderloin flat on a work surface. Arrange the fruit on the pork. Crumble the chèvre cheese on top. Bring the two sides together and lay on one side. Using cotton kitchen string, bind the tenderloin every inch or so then cut the ties back to ¼ inch. Combine the olive oil and chèvre. Coat the tenderloin with it before seasoning with salt and pepper. Place on the barbecue over moderately high heat. Cook the tenderloin until the outside is browned but the inside is no longer pink. Slice into medallions about 1-inch thick and serve with the port sauce. Serves 4.

GINGER BUTTERFLIED LEG OF LAMB

3 tbsp	soy sauce
½ cup	hoisin sauce
¼ cup	rice wine vinegar
1 tbsp	fresh ginger, peeled and grated
2 tbsp	fresh mint, finely cut
4 cloves	garlic, peeled and minced
¼ cup	scallions, chopped
1 tbsp	honey
1 6-lb	leg of lamb, boned and butterflied

Combine the soy sauce, hoisin sauce, rice wine vinegar, ginger, mint, garlic, scallions, and honey in a large dish big enough to accommodate the lamb. Add the lamb and toss to coat. Let marinate about 1 hour at room temperature. Remove the lamb from the marinade and pat dry to prevent flare ups. Place on the grill over moderately high heat and cook about 10 minutes a side until the lamb is nicely browned and the inside is still pink. Remove from the grill and let stand about 5 minutes tented with foil. Cut into ½-inch slices and serve. Serves 6.

Herb-Crusted Center-Cut Pork Chops with Royal Gala Apples

¼ cup	olive oil
2 tbsp	balsamic vinegar
1 tsp	Dijon mustard
1 stick	cinnamon, 4 inches long, broken in 4 pieces
4	Royal Gala apples
8	center-cut, boneless pork chops
1 cup	fresh bread crumbs
1 tbsp	fresh thyme, finely chopped
1 tbsp	fresh sage, finely chopped
1 tbsp	fresh parsley, finely chopped
½ cup	Parmesan cheese, finely grated
2 tbsp	butter, softened
1 tsp	Dijon mustard
	salt and pepper
	cinnamon for sprinkling

Combine the olive oil, vinegar, mustard, and cinnamon sticks in a dish big enough to accommodate the pork chops and apples. Cut the apples in half. Using a melon baller, remove the cores from the apples. Trim ends. Cut in half again and place in the marinade. Add the pork and toss everything until well-coated. Combine the bread crumbs, herbs, cheese, butter, mustard, and seasoning. Work the ingredients by hand until well-blended. Place the pork chops and apples on the grill over high heat and cook until the apples are browned and tender, and the pork is browned on one side and seared on the other. Place the pork on a work surface, seared side down, then press the bread crumb mixture onto the surface of the chops. Return the chops to the grill and barbecue with the lid down for another 5 minutes or so. Remove the apples to a serving dish when done and immediately sprinkle with a little cinnamon. Serve the pork chops with the apples on the side. Serves 4.

HONEY-BASIL PORK

½ cup	honey
2 tbsp	lemon juice
¼ cup	soya sauce
4 cloves	garlic, crushed
2 tbsp	fresh basil, finely cut
2 tbsp	fresh parsley, chopped
2	pork tenderloin, cut in half lengthwise

Combine honey, lemon juice, soya sauce, garlic, basil, and parsley in a small bowl and mix well. Add the pork and marinate 1 hour at room temperature or overnight in the refrigerator. Grill the tenderloin over high heat, brushing with the marinade, and turning as needed until they are brown on all sides and just pink on the inside. Serves 4.

HONEY-GINGER STEAK WITH FRESH FRUIT CHUTNEY

¼ cup	white vinegar
2 tbsp	honey
1	peach, peeled, pitted and chopped
4	plums, pitted and chopped
12	cherries, pitted and halved
⅓ cup	fresh mint, finely cut
1	red pepper, seeded and chopped
½	jalapeño pepper, seeded, deveined, and minced
1 tbsp	fresh ginger, peeled and minced
1 clove	garlic, peeled and minced
½ cup	soya sauce
¼ cup	honey
¼ cup	balsamic vinegar
3 tbsp	fresh ginger, peeled and coarsely grated
2 cloves	garlic (large), peeled and crushed
4	New York strip sirloin steaks
4 sprigs	fresh mint (for garnish)
	fresh fruit chutney

Combine vinegar, honey, peach, plums, cherries, mint, red pepper, jalapeño pepper, ginger, and garlic. Let the chutney sit for at least 30 minutes. If made ahead, refrigerate up to 4 hours. The fruit is not at its best if made too far in advance.

Combine soya sauce, honey, balsamic vinegar, ginger, garlic in a dish, then add the steaks. Let the steaks marinate for 1 hour at room temperature or up to 24 hours in the refrigerator. Grill the steaks over high heat, brushing with the marinade, and turning as needed until brown on the outside, but still pink on the inside. Serve with the fresh chutney. Garnish with the mint. Serves 4.

Horseradish Lamb Tenderloins

½ cup	yogurt
1 tbsp	prepared horseradish
1 tbsp	fresh rosemary, chopped
4 cloves	garlic, peeled and minced
1 tbsp	lime juice
	salt and pepper
4	boneless lamb tenderloins

Combine the yogurt, horseradish, rosemary, garlic, lime juice, salt, and pepper to make a marinade. Reserve half of the marinade in a small serving dish. Add the tenderloins to the remaining marinade and let sit at room temperature for 30 minutes. Place on the grill over medium high heat and cook about 10 minutes, turning on four sides until the lamb is browned on the outside and barely pink on the inside. Serve with a dollop of the yogurt mixture. Serves 4.

LAMB WITH MINT PESTO

⅓ cup	walnuts
6 cloves	garlic, peeled
2 cups	fresh mint leaves
¼ cup	olive oil
¼ cup	balsamic vinegar
1	boneless, butterflied leg of lamb
	olive oil
4 cloves	garlic, peeled
	salt and pepper

Combine walnuts, garlic, mint, olive oil, and balsamic vinegar in the bowl of a food processor fitted with a steel blade and process until the mixture is well combined, but still coarse. Set pesto aside.

Flatten the thickest parts of the lamb by pounding with a mallet. Cut 8 slits in the lamb. Cut the four garlic cloves in half lengthwise and place one in each slit. Brush with olive oil, season with salt and pepper, then place over high heat. Cook, turning and brushing as needed, until browned on the outside, but still pink on the inside, about 10 minutes a side.

Serve the lamb with the pesto. Serves 6 to 8 as a main course, or 25 plus as an hors d'oeuvre.

Lamb with Mustard and Herbs

1	boneless leg of lamb
½ cup	olive oil
1½ tbsp	fennel
1½ tbsp	rosemary
1½ tbsp	mint
2 tsp	Dijon mustard
	salt and pepper

Lay the lamb flat on a work surface and pound with a mallet until the meat is less than 1 inch thick. Combine the olive oil, fennel, rosemary, mint, mustard, salt, and pepper in a dish and add the lamb. Turn to coat and let rest for 30 minutes. Place on the barbecue over high heat and cook, turning as needed, until the lamb is browned on the outside, but still pink on the inside. Test with your finger for doneness. The meat should have some give to it. Let stand for 5 minutes. Slice about ¼ inch thick. Serve with its juices. Serves 8.

Lamb Tenderloins with Hot Red Pepper Relish

2 tbsp	olive oil
4 cloves	garlic, peeled and mashed
	salt and pepper
4	lamb tenderloins
2 cups	red peppers, seeded and cut in ½-inch dice
½ cups	red onion, peeled and finely chopped
½ cup	apple cider vinegar
2 tbsp	honey
½ tsp	Dijon mustard
2	chipotle chilies in adobo sauce, minced
	salt and pepper

Combine the olive oil and garlic, and add the lamb tenderloins. Season with salt and pepper. Let sit about 1 hour at room temperature.

Meanwhile, combine the red pepper, onion, vinegar, honey, mustard, and chipotle chilies in a saucepan over moderate heat. When the mixture begins to simmer, reduce heat to low and simmer ingredients for about 40 minutes, until they are tender and the liquid has evaporated. Season with salt and pepper. Set aside and reheat before serving.

Place lamb on the barbecue over moderately high heat and cook until the lamb is browned on the outside, but still pink inside. Serve with the relish. Serves 6.

Nancy's Chili-Tequila Ribs

2 racks	spare ribs
1	coarsely chopped onion
¾ cup	hot water
1 tbsp	crushed hot chilies
½ cup	ketchup
3 cloves	garlic
½ cup	cider vinegar
2 tbsp	brown sugar
2 tsp	salt
⅓ cup	tequila
½ cup	vegetable oil
½ tsp	ground cumin
⅓ tsp	ground allspice

Put spareribs and onion in a large pot and cover with cold water. Bring water to a boil. Cover and let ribs simmer for 50 minutes. Drain and place ribs on a platter long enough to accommodate them.

Combine water, chilies, ketchup, garlic, cider vinegar, brown sugar, salt, tequila, vegetable oil, cumin, and allspice in a blender or food processor. Process until well-combined. Pour the mixture over the ribs and marinate for several hours or overnight in the refrigerator.

Place the ribs on the barbecue over moderately high heat and cook, brushing with the marinade until nicely glazed, about 6 minutes on each side.

Meanwhile, in a small saucepan over moderate heat on the side burner of the barbecue, bring the remaining marinade to a boil. Reduce heat to low and let simmer for several minutes. Serve with the ribs. Serves 6.

Nancy's Thai-Marinated Pork Chops

4	center-cut pork chops
¼ cup	nam plah (Vietnamese fish sauce)
3 tbsp	lime juice
2 tbsp	vegetable oil
2 tbsp	sugar
2 cloves	garlic
1 inch	fresh ginger, peeled and minced
1 tsp	Thai curry paste or crushed hot chilies
½ cup	fresh cilantro

Place pork chops in a zip-lock bag or shallow dish. Put nam plah, lime juice, vegetable oil, sugar, garlic, ginger, Thai curry paste, and cilantro in a food processor and purée. Pour the mixture over the pork chops and marinate about 20 minutes at room temperature or overnight in the refrigerator.

Place the chops on the barbecue over high heat and cook, brushing with the marinade several times until just barely pink on the inside, about 4 minutes a side. Serves 4.

OLD-FASHIONED BARBECUE SPARERIBS

This recipe has been in the family for years. It was one of the first dinner recipes that I ever mastered and I wooed my future husband with it.

3-4 lbs	pork spareribs
½ cup	onion, peeled and chopped
2 tbsp	butter
1 cup	water
¼ cup	vinegar
2½ tbsp	Worcestershire sauce
½ cup	lemon juice
¼ cup	brown sugar
2 cups	bottled chili sauce
1 tsp	salt
¾ tsp	paprika

Cut the ribs into serving-size pieces. Place in a roasting pan, cover with foil and bake at 450°F for 15 minutes. Brown the onions in the melted butter. Add water, vinegar, Worcestershire sauce, lemon juice, brown sugar, chili sauce, salt, and paprika, then let simmer for 20 minutes. Brush the ribs with the barbecue sauce and place over moderately high heat. Brush and turn frequently, until ribs are cooked to taste. Serves 6.

Paprika Pork with King Eringle Mushrooms

Any mushrooms will do here but, as these ones are so beautiful, when they are available, I like to use them.

⅓ cup	olive oil
1 lb	King Eringle mushrooms
⅓ cup	onions, peeled and minced
1 cup	red wine
	salt and pepper
2	pork tenderloins
¼ cup	olive oil
4 cloves	garlic, peeled and minced
1 tbsp	Hungarian paprika
	salt and pepper

Heat the olive oil in a medium skillet over moderately high heat on the side burner of the barbecue. Add the mushrooms and the onions, and cook until the juices begin to dry up. Stir the wine in and turn up the heat to high. Reduce to about ⅓ cup of liquid. Season with salt and pepper.

Place the pork in a dish with the olive oil, garlic, paprika, and seasoning. Toss to coat and let stand for 30 minutes. Turn and let stand another 30 minutes. Place on the barbecue over moderately high heat and grill on four sides until nicely browned, but still barely pink on the inside. Let stand for about 5 minutes. Slice into pieces about an inch thick and serve on top of the mushrooms. Serves 4.

PINK PEPPERCORN PORK LOIN STEAKS

8	boneless pork loin steaks
¼ cup	pink peppercorns
	salt and pepper
	olive oil for grilling

Crush the peppercorns in a mortar with pestle, or in a plastic bag with a mallet, or with a rolling pin. Press them onto both sides of the pork steaks, season with salt and pepper, and place them on the grill over moderately high heat. Spray or carefully brush the steaks with a little olive oil, trying not to disturb the pink peppercorns. Cook, turning and spraying until browned on the outside, but still slightly pink on the inside. Serves 4.

Pork with Curried Mango Avocado and Banana Salsa

1	mango, peeled and cut in ½-inch dice
1	avocado, peeled and cut in ½-inch dice
1	small red onion, peeled and chopped
3 tbsp	olive oil
3 tbsp	freshly squeezed orange juice
1 tbsp	freshly squeezed lime juice
2 tbsp	white wine vinegar
2 tsp	curry powder
1 tbsp	fresh mint, finely chopped
3	pork tenderloins
¼ cup	olive oil
1 tsp	curry powder
	salt and pepper
1	banana, peeled and cut in ½-inch dice

Combine the mango, avocado, onion, olive oil, juices, vinegar, curry powder, and mint in a medium bowl. Mix well and refrigerate.

Put the ¼ cup olive oil and curry powder in a small dish and brush the pork tenderloins with it. Season them with salt and pepper. Place the tenderloins on the grill over moderately high heat and cook them, turning and brushing as needed, until nicely browned on the outside, but still pink on the inside. Let the tenderloins rest for a few minutes. Add the banana to the salsa. Slice the tenderloins and serve with the salsa. Serves 6.

Pork with Curry-Honey-Mustard Glaze

⅓ cup   honey
½ cup   granular Dijon mustard
1 tbsp   curry powder
    salt and pepper
2   pork tenderloins

Combine the honey, mustard, curry powder, salt, and pepper in a dish, and add the pork tenderloins. Marinate for about 30 minutes at room temperature. Place on the grill over moderately high heat and cook, turning and basting as needed until the pork is nicely browned on the outside, but just barely pink on the inside, about 20 minutes. Serves 4.

PORK TENDERLOIN WITH SPICY TOMATO JAM

6	plum tomatoes
¼ cup	brown sugar
⅓ cup	balsamic vinegar
4 cloves	garlic, peeled and minced
2 sticks	cinnamon, 2 inches long
1	whole nutmeg
1	shallot, peeled and stuck with 2 whole cloves
1	star anise pod
	salt and pepper
3	pork tenderloins

One at a time, plunge the tomatoes into a pot of boiling water for 10 seconds each and then peel. Chop the tomatoes and place them in a medium saucepan over high heat on the side burner of the barbecue. Add the brown sugar, vinegar, garlic, cinnamon sticks, nutmeg, shallot with whole cloves, star anise, salt, and pepper, then bring to a boil. Reduce heat to medium-low and simmer until the mixture has thickened, about 20 minutes. Remove the shallot with the cloves and the other whole spices. Set aside and keep warm or reheat before serving.

Meanwhile, brush the pork tenderloins with olive oil and sprinkle with salt and pepper. Place them over moderately high heat on the barbecue and cook, turning and brushing as needed, until the pork is browned on the outside, but still a little pink on the inside. Cut the tenderloins into ½-inch medallions and serve with the spicy tomato jam. Serves 6.

Rabbit with Yogurt and Rosemary

¼ cup	olive oil
4 cloves	garlic, peeled and minced
2 tbsp	lemon juice
1 cup	yogurt
¼ cup	rosemary leaves, chopped
	salt and pepper
1	rabbit, cut into 6 serving pieces

Combine olive oil, garlic, lemon juice, yogurt, rosemary, salt, and pepper in a dish. Add the rabbit and toss to coat. Marinate for about 4 hours in the refrigerator. Place on the barbecue over moderately high heat and cook, turning as needed until the rabbit is no longer pink on the inside. Serves 6.

RED PEPPER JELLY PORK

1 cup	red pepper jelly
2 tbsp	lemon juice
2 tbsp	fresh lemon rind, grated
2 tbsp	fresh tarragon, minced
2 tbsp	olive oil
6 cloves	garlic, peeled and minced
3	pork tenderloins
	salt and pepper

Melt the jelly in a small saucepan on the side burner of the barbecue over moderately high heat. Add the lemon juice, lemon rind, tarragon, olive oil, and garlic. Cook for about 1 minute then remove from heat. Place a little more than half of the mixture in a small bowl and set aside.

Season the pork tenderloins with salt and pepper, place in a dish, and coat with the remaining red pepper jelly sauce. Place the tenderloins on the barbecue over moderately high heat. Brush often with the marinade, turning as needed. Cook until the meat is nicely browned on the outside, but still barely pink on the inside. Let stand for 5 minutes, tented with foil. Slice about ½ inch thick and serve with the reserved sauce. Serves 6.

Roast Beef with Beaujolais Sauce

The sauce may take as long as an hour to make, so plan to start it about halfway through the cooking time of the roast beef.

3½–4 lbs	prime rib roast of beef
1 tbsp	olive oil
2	carrots, peeled and finely chopped
2	celery stalks, finely chopped
1	onion, peeled and finely chopped
3 cloves	garlic, peeled and minced
3 sprigs	thyme
1 cup	beef stock
4 cups	good red Beaujolais wine
	salt and pepper
1 tbsp	butter
1 tbsp	flour
8 strips	loin steaks

Place the roast beef on one side of the barbecue over high heat. Close the lid, turn the burner off under the roast, and turn the other burner to moderately low. Cook the roast until medium rare, about 140°F or less on a meat thermometer, about 2 hours. Let the roast sit on a warm platter tented with foil for about 30 minutes.

Heat the olive oil in a medium skillet on the side burner of the barbecue over moderate heat. Add the carrots, celery, onion, garlic, and thyme, and cook until tender. Add the red wine and let simmer until the sauce is reduced to about 1 cup. Add the beef broth and reduce again to about 1 cup.

Mix the flour and butter together into a paste. Add a tablespoon of the sauce. Stir to combine. Put the mixture back into the sauce. Stir and simmer for another few minutes. Serve the roast beef with the Beaujolais sauce. Serves 8.

Rosemary Steak with Goat Cheese Mashed Potatoes

9	medium russet potatoes, peeled and halved
¼ cup	butter
1	onion, peeled and chopped
¾ cup	milk
¼ cup	chèvre cheese, crumbled
	salt and pepper
6	T-bone steaks
2 tbsp	fresh rosemary leaves, minced
1 tbsp	olive oil
	salt and pepper

Place the potatoes in a pot of salted, boiling water and set on the side burner of the barbecue over moderately high heat. Cover and cook until very tender, about 20 to 30 minutes. Drain and keep warm.

Meanwhile, heat the butter in a medium skillet over moderate heat and add the onions. Cook until softened and just beginning to brown. Add the milk and bring almost to the boil. Add the mixture, along with the chèvre cheese to the potatoes. Mash. Season with salt and pepper. Set aside and keep warm.

Meanwhile, crush the minced rosemary leaves to release more of their oil. Add the olive oil. Brush the steaks lightly with the mixture and season them with salt and pepper. Place steaks on the barbecue over high heat and cook, until browned on the outside and pink on the inside, about 8 minutes. Let stand, tented with foil, for about 5 minutes and serve on a bed of chèvre mashed potatoes with any accumulated juices from the platter. Serves 6.

Shelagh's Raspberry Vinegar Lamb

This is a recipe from the queen of indirect grilling. She has a court full of followers, including me.

1 tsp	pink peppercorns
1 tsp	green peppercorns
1 tsp	white peppercorns
1 tsp	Jamaican peppercorns
¼ tsp	whole allspice
¼ cup	extra virgin olive oil
3 tbsp	raspberry vinegar
3 cloves	garlic, peeled and crushed
1 tbsp	fresh rosemary leaves, crushed
2 tsp	Dijon mustard
1	boneless leg of lamb, butterflied

Combine the 4 kinds of peppercorns and the allspice in a mortar with pestle. Grind into a coarse powder. Place the mixture in a small bowl then add the olive oil, vinegar, garlic, rosemary, and Dijon. Mix well and rub onto the surface of the lamb. Place the lamb on the barbecue over high heat and sear quickly on both sides. Turn one burner to low heat and put the lamb on the other side of the grill. Close the lid of the barbecue and turn the burner off under the lamb. Cook, turning and basting, until the lamb is browned on the outside, but still pink inside, about 45 minutes to 1 hour. Serves 6.

SIRLOIN STEAK WITH MERLOT BUTTER ON POTATO PANCAKES

1 tbsp	olive oil
2 cloves	garlic, peeled and minced
1 cup	Merlot wine
1 tsp	fresh thyme leaves
½ cup	butter
1	large sirloin steak, 1½ inches thick, cut into 6 portions
	olive oil for grilling
	salt and pepper
6	potato pancakes

Put the olive oil in a small saucepan on the side burner of the barbecue over moderate heat. Add the garlic and cook about 30 seconds. Add the wine and raise the heat to high. Cook until the wine mixture is reduced to about 2 tbsp. Cool to room temperature. Place the butter in a food processor. Add the wine mixture and the thyme and process until smooth. Place on a piece of waxed paper, form into a log, wrap tightly, and chill about 2 hours.

Brush the steaks with olive oil, then season with salt and pepper. Place the steaks on the barbecue over high heat. Cook until browned on both sides. Turn the heat down to moderate and cook to medium rare or desired doneness. Let the steaks stand, tented with foil, about 5 minutes. Cut the log of butter into disks. Serve immediately on top of a potato pancake with a disk of the Merlot butter on top. Serves 6.

POTATO PANCAKES

6	potatoes, peeled and grated
2 tbsp	chives, finely chopped
4	green onions, finely chopped
	salt and pepper
	butter and olive oil for frying

Combine the potatoes, chives, green onions, salt and pepper, and mix well. Heat a little butter and olive oil in a medium skillet over moderately high heat on the side burner of the barbecue. Scoop portions of the batter into the skillet and flatten to form a pancake about ½ inch thick. Cook until golden brown on the bottom and turn, about 6 minutes. Cook the other side until golden, about another 6 to 8 minutes. If the inside of the pancake still seems unfinished, keep turning until done.

SPICY RACK OF LAMB WITH MAPLE MUSTARD GLAZE

4 racks	lamb
½ cup	olive oil
3 tbsp	cider vinegar
1 tsp	cinnamon
1 tsp	ginger
½ tsp	nutmeg
	salt and pepper
⅔ cup	Dijon mustard
3 tbsp	maple syrup

Trim all the meat and fat from the extended tips of the rib bones, so that they are clean down to the loin portion of the rack. Cover the exposed bone portion of the racks with foil if desired.

Combine the olive oil, cider vinegar, cinnamon, ginger, nutmeg, salt, and pepper in a small bowl. Brush the mixture on the racks and let stand for about 1 hour. Place the racks on the barbecue over moderately high heat and cook, turning, for about 20 minutes, until browned on the outside, but not quite finished cooking. Combine the Dijon mustard and the maple syrup in a small dish and start basting the lamb with it. Continue to cook, basting frequently until the inside of the racks is cooked through but still pink, about 20 minutes. Remove the foil wrappers for the last 5 minutes or so of cooking. Serves 4.

Steak with Swiss Chard and Cabernet Sauvignon Butter

1 tbsp	olive oil
1 tsp	garlic, peeled and minced
1 cup	Cabernet Sauvignon wine
½ cup	butter
4	filet mignon steaks, cut 1-inch thick
	olive oil for grilling
	salt and pepper
2 bunches	red Swiss chard
½ cup	water
3 tbsp	olive oil
4 cloves	garlic, peeled and minced
	salt and pepper

Heat the olive oil in a medium saucepan over moderate heat, add the garlic, and cook about 30 seconds. Add the wine. Turn the heat to high and cook, stirring occasionally, until reduced to about 2 tbsp. Cool and place in the bowl of a food processor. Add the butter and process until smooth. Put the mixture on a piece of wax paper and form into a log. Wrap and chill for an hour or so.

Brush the steaks with olive oil then season with salt and pepper. Put the steaks on the barbecue over high heat and cook until they are browned on the outside and still pink inside, about 8 minutes.

Meanwhile, place the Swiss chard and water in a large skillet over high heat on the side burner of the barbecue. Cook until the Swiss chard has wilted and the water has evaporated. Immediately add the olive oil and garlic. Stir and cook about 2 minutes until the garlic has browned. Remove the skillet from the heat and season with salt and pepper. Serve the steak on a bed of the Swiss chard with a disk of the Cabernet Sauvignon butter on top. Serves 4.

Strip Loin Steak and Mushrooms on Beaujolais Mashed Potatoes

6	potatoes, peeled and halved
2 tsp	olive oil
2 cloves	garlic
½ cup	Beaujolais red wine
¼ cup	potato water
2 tbsp	whipping cream
3 tbsp	butter
	salt and pepper
4 strip	loin steaks
	olive oil for grilling
	salt and pepper
2 tbsp	olive oil
1 lb	mushrooms, sliced
	salt and pepper

Place the potatoes in a pot of water to cover and bring to a boil. Reduce the heat a little and cook until tender, about 20 to 30 minutes. Drain the potatoes, reserving the cooking water. Measure about ⅓ cup and return it to the pot of potatoes.

Meanwhile, pour the olive oil into a small saucepan, place over moderate heat, and add the garlic. Cook about 30 seconds, then add the wine. Cook until the mixture is reduced to 2 tbsp. Add the wine reduction, cream, butter, salt, and pepper to the potatoes. Mash and cover to keep warm.

Brush the steaks with a little olive oil, season with salt and pepper, and place on the grill over high heat. Cook 4 to 6 minutes a side, depending on the thickness of the steaks. Let rest 5 minutes tented with foil.

Meanwhile, heat the 2 tbsp olive oil in a skillet over moderately high heat on the side burner of the barbecue. Add the mushrooms. Cook, stirring occasionally, until the pan juices have begun to dry up and the mushrooms are nicely browned. Season with salt and pepper. Serve the steak on a bed of mashed potatoes, topped with the mushrooms. Drizzle with any accumulated juices from the steak platter. Serves 4.

POULTRY

THE MOST DURABLE GRILL
KNOWN TO MAN

Big Al's Thai Grilled Chicken

Alison buys her ingredients at an Asian market. The red Vietnamese chili sauce, unlike Sambal Oelek, is an oil-based mixture with little chilies in it.

5 tbsp	nam plah (Vietnamese fish sauce)
¼ cup	light brown sugar
¼ cup	canned, unsweetened coconut milk
2 tbsp	lime juice
2 tbsp	five-spice powder
2 tbsp	soy sauce
1 tbsp	crushed dried Asian chilies
1 tbsp	curry powder
2 3-lb	chickens, quartered, rinsed, and dried
	cooked rice for 8
1	red onion, peeled and chopped
2	tomatoes, chopped
1	cucumber, peeled and chopped
8	butter lettuce leaves
	dipping sauce

Combine the nam plah, brown sugar, coconut milk, lime juice, five-spice powder, soy sauce, Asian chilies, and curry powder, then add the chicken. Turn every 12 hours for 2 days. Grill the chicken pieces over high heat quickly to seal in the juices for about 2 minutes a side. Reduce the heat to moderate and cook, turning and basting as needed, until the juices run clear when pierced with a fork, about 20 minutes. Serve with rice, chopped red onions, tomatoes, and cucumber on a large leaf of butter lettuce with dipping sauce (recipe on following page). Serves 8.

DIPPING SAUCE
for Big Al's Thai Grilled Chicken

1½ cups	rice wine vinegar
¾ cup	sugar
2 tbsp	garlic, peeled and minced
1 tbsp	red Vietnamese chili sauce

Combine the ingredients. Let stand 2 hours. Strain and serve.

CHICKEN BREASTS WITH MUSTARD SEED MARINADE

6	skinless, boneless chicken breasts
2 tbsp	mustard seeds
1½ tbsp	fresh ginger, peeled and grated
1 clove	garlic, peeled and minced
½ cup	fresh cilantro, chopped
¼ cup	fresh parsley, chopped
2 tsp	grated lime zest
3 tbsp	fresh lime juice
⅓ cup	olive oil
2 tbsp	wine vinegar
1 tsp	hot sauce
	salt and pepper

Toast the mustard seeds in a small skillet over moderate heat until slightly browned, about 2 minutes. In a dish big enough to accommodate the chicken breasts, combine all the ingredients then add the chicken. Turn to coat and let marinate for about an hour at room temperature. Grill the chicken breasts over high heat, brushing with marinade and turning as needed. Serves 6.

Chicken Fajitas

½ cup	olive oil
1 tbsp	red wine vinegar
¼ cup	soya sauce
2 tsp	Worcestershire sauce
3 tsp	garlic, peeled and crushed
2 tsp	Tabasco sauce
1½ tsp	dry mustard
1 tsp	freshly ground black pepper
8	boneless chicken breast halves
2 tbsp	olive oil
	guacamole
	tomato salsa
	sour cream
1	red pepper, seed and sliced into wide strips
2	medium onions, peeled and sliced thickly
8	fresh soft tortillas

Combine olive oil, red wine vinegar, soya sauce, Worcestershire sauce, garlic, Tabasco sauce, dry mustard, black pepper. Marinate for 1 hour at room temperature or overnight in the refrigerator. Brown the peppers and onions in 2 tbsp olive oil until softened and slightly brown. Barbecue the chicken over high heat, brushing with the marinade, and turning as needed, until the inside is no longer pink and the outside is nicely brown. Remove to a platter and slice the chicken breasts thinly. Serve with bowls of guacamole, salsa, sour cream, plus the peppers and onion. Pile the ingredients onto warmed soft tortillas, then roll up to eat. Serves 4.

Guacamole

1	ripe avocado
2 tsp	lime juice
1 tbsp	fresh cilantro, finely chopped
1 tbsp	onion, finely chopped
	hot pepper and sauce to taste
¼ tsp	salt

Cut the avocado in half and remove the pit. Scoop out the flesh. Mash the avocado and add the lime juice, cilantro, onion, tomato, hot pepper sauce, and salt. Mix well and cover. Chill in the refrigerator if serving later. Yields approximately 1 cup.

Salsa

5	tomatoes
¼ cup	green onions, chopped
⅓ cup	fresh cilantro, chopped
½	jalapeño pepper, seeded and minced
1 tbsp	olive oil
1 tbsp	lime juice
2 cloves	garlic, minced
	salt and pepper

Combine green onions, cilantro, jalapeño pepper, olive oil, lime juice, garlic, salt, and pepper, then let sit for 30 minutes at room temperature. Cover and refrigerate if serving later. Try not to make more than 2 hours ahead of time.

Chicken with Grilled Eggplant Salsa

1	eggplant
1	tomato, cut into ½-inch dice
1	yellow pepper, cut into ½-inch dice
½ cup	black olives, pitted and cut
1 tbsp	fresh rosemary leaves, minced
2 tbsp	olive oil
2 tbsp	fresh lemon juice
	salt and pepper
6	skinless, boneless chicken breast halves
¼ cup	olive oil
2 tbsp	fresh lemon juice

Place the whole eggplant on the grill over moderately high heat, turning as the skin blackens. Cook until the entire skin is black and the inside is soft. Cool. Remove as much of the charred skin as possible. Split the eggplant in half and remove the seedy sections. Cut the eggplant in 1-inch dice. Drain the cubes in a colander until most of the liquid has been released. Place in a bowl with the tomato, yellow pepper, olives, and rosemary. Stir in the oil, lemon juice, and seasoning. Combine well.

Trim the chicken breasts of excess fat. Combine the olive oil and lemon juice, then coat the chicken with it. Place on the barbecue over high heat. Grill about 4 to 5 minutes a side, until browned on the outside and no longer pink on the inside. Serve with the eggplant salsa. Serves 6.

CHICKEN LEGS WITH BROWN SUGAR SPICE RUB

4	chicken legs
1 tbsp	coriander seeds
2 tbsp	cumin seeds
1 tbsp	dark brown sugar
1 tsp	kosher salt
2 tsp	cinnamon
1 tsp	cayenne pepper
1 tsp	black pepper, freshly ground

Toast the coriander and cumin seeds in a small skillet over moderate heat until fragrant. Combine the brown sugar with the other ingredients in a mortar and work with the pestle until they are finely ground. Work the mixture into the skin of the chicken legs with your fingers. Grill over moderate heat, so that the skin does not burn before the chicken is cooked inside. Turn as needed. Serves 4.

Chicken with Red Pepper Basmati Rice Pudding

1 tbsp	olive oil
¼ cup	onion, finely chopped
3 cloves	garlic, peeled and minced
½ cup	red pepper, seeded and finely chopped
1 cup	cooked basmati rice
1 egg	
⅔ cup	milk
1 tbsp	olive oil
½ tsp	cayenne pepper
4	boneless chicken breasts
	salt and pepper

Heat the olive oil in a small saucepan over moderate heat and add onion. Cook until the onion has softened before adding garlic. Cook until the garlic is beginning to brown then add the red pepper. Continue cooking until the pepper has softened. Cool the mixture for a few minutes, then place in a small baking dish. Add the rice, egg, milk, butter, salt, and pepper. Bake in a 325°F oven until set or a paring knife inserted in the pudding comes out clean, about 20 to 25 minutes.

Meanwhile, combine the olive oil with the cayenne pepper and brush on the chicken breasts. Season with salt and pepper before placing on the grill over high heat. Cook, turning as needed, until no longer pink on the inside. Serve with the rice pudding. Serves 4.

Cinnamon Chicken

½ cup	olive oil
1 tbsp	ground cinnamon
	salt and pepper
6	boneless chicken breasts

Combine the olive oil and cinnamon in a dish big enough to accommodate the chicken and mix well. Add the chicken breasts. Toss to coat. Cover and refrigerate overnight. Place on the grill over moderately high heat, skin-side down. Cook on each side until both sides are browned and the inside of the chicken is no longer pink. Serves 6.

Cocoa-Dusted Duck on Potatoes with Red Currant Sauce

2 tbsp	olive oil
4 cloves	garlic, peeled and minced
2 cups	red wine
¼ cup	red currant jelly
	salt and pepper
1 tbsp	cocoa
	salt and pepper
4	duck breasts
2 large	Yukon Gold potatoes, cut in ½-inch slices
2 tbsp	butter
	salt and pepper

Heat the olive oil in a medium saucepan over moderate heat and add the garlic. Cook about 30 seconds and add the wine. Raise the heat to high and cook until reduced to about ¼ cup. Add the red currant jelly and stir to combine. Remove from the heat and season with salt and pepper. Set aside and keep warm.

Sprinkle the cocoa, salt, and pepper on the duck breasts then rub into the surface of the duck. Place the duck on the barbecue over moderately high heat. Turn the burner off under the duck breasts and cook indirectly. Turn as needed and cook until the breasts have browned and the interior of the duck is no longer pink.

Meanwhile, place the potato slices on a piece of barbecue-strength foil. Dot the slices with the butter and sprinkle with salt and pepper. Wrap the foil into a tightly sealed package and place on the barbecue over moderately high heat, on the side with the live burner. Cook until the potatoes are tender, about 20 to 30 minutes. Serve each breast on a potato slice with a little sauce. Serves 4.

Cornish Hens Stuffed with Wild Rice and Dried Fruit Stuffing

½ cup	wild rice
4 cups	water
2 tbsp	butter
¼ cup	onion
¼ cup	dried cherries
¼ cup	dried blueberries
¼ cup	dried apricots, chopped
1 tsp	fresh thyme leaves
	salt and pepper
½ cup	peach jam
4 tsp	white balsamic vinegar
4	Cornish hens, weighing about 1-1½ lbs each
8	small sprigs thyme
	olive oil for grilling

Slowly add the wild rice to the boiling water and return to the boil. Cover and reduce heat to moderately low so that the mixture simmers constantly. Cook until the grains of rice begin to puff and pop open, about 50 to 60 minutes. Fluff with a fork, let stand for 5 minutes, and drain excess water. Place in a bowl.

Heat the butter over moderate heat in a small saucepan and add the onion. Cook until softened, about 4 minutes. Add the mixture to the wild rice, along with the dried fruit, thyme, salt, and pepper. Combine well and set aside.

Heat the peach jam and balsamic vinegar in a small saucepan over moderate heat. Strain into a small bowl and set aside.

Rinse the hens, inside and out, then pat dry with paper towels. Sprinkle the main cavity with a little salt and pepper. Slip your finger under the skin of the hen just above the cavity to make a little pocket. Tuck some sprigs of thyme under the skin and pat it back into place. Spoon wild rice stuffing into the main cavity of the hens. Truss the two legs and the tail portion together with cotton kitchen string. Turn the bird over and spoon stuffing into the neck cavity. Stretch the skin down over the stuffing and tuck the tips of the wings back behind the body of the bird, helping to hold the stretched skin in place. Brush the hens with olive oil, season with salt and pepper, and place on one side of the grill over moderate heat. Lower barbecue lid and turn the burner off under the hens. Cook, turning, rotating, and basting the hens about every 15 minutes, until the leg juices run clear when pierced with a skewer, about 90 minutes. Move the hens over to the hot side of the barbecue, turn the burner to high, and brush with the peach glaze, turning once, for the last few minutes of cooking. Serves 4.

Duck Breasts on Herb Bread Pudding with Concord Grape Sauce

6 tbsp	butter
4 cloves	garlic, peeled and minced
¼ cup	red onion, peeled and minced
2 cups	milk
4	eggs
2 tbsp	fresh parsley, minced
1 tbsp	fresh thyme leaves
1 tbsp	fresh sage leaves, minced
	salt and pepper
6 oz	stale French bread, torn into pieces
1 tbsp	butter
2 cloves	garlic, peeled and minced
2 cups	red wine
1 stick	cinnamon, 4 inches long
1 tbsp	mint leaves, minced
¼ cup	Concord grape jelly
	salt and pepper
6	duck breasts
	olive oil for grilling
	salt and pepper

Heat the butter in a small saucepan over moderate heat then add the garlic and onion. Cook until they are softened. Pour the melted butter mixture into an oven-proof baking dish then add the milk, eggs, herbs, salt, and pepper. Add the bread, stir, and let sit for about 30 minutes. Cover the pudding with tin foil and set it in a roasting pan filled with boiling water in the middle of a

350°F oven. Bake for 30 minutes. Remove the foil and bake for another 20 minutes, until just set. Keep warm.

Meanwhile, heat the olive oil over moderate heat on the side burner of the barbecue and add the garlic. Cook for about 30 seconds then add the red wine, cinnamon stick, and mint. Raise the heat to high and cook until the sauce is reduced to ½ cup. Add the grape jelly and cook, stirring constantly, until the sauce thickens. Season with salt and pepper. Keep warm or reheat before serving.

Brush the duck breast with a little olive oil then season with salt and pepper. Place them over moderately high heat on the barbecue. Cook until the duck is browned nicely and no longer pink on the inside, about 7 minutes a side. Serve with a dollop of the herb bread pudding and a spoonful of the Concord grape sauce on top. Serves 6.

Ginger Chicken Drumsticks

¼ cup	fresh ginger, grated
2 cloves	garlic, peeled and minced
⅓ cup	teriyaki sauce
3 tbsp	olive oil
	salt and pepper
8	chicken drumsticks

Put ginger, garlic, teriyaki sauce, olive oil, salt, and pepper in a bowl and stir until well-combined. Rub the paste on the chicken legs and let them sit, covered in the refrigerator, for 30 minutes. Place on the grill over moderate heat and cook, turning as needed, until the chicken is no longer pink inside, about 20 or 30 minutes. Serves 4.

HERB-PACKED TURKEY BREAST WITH MANGO CHUTNEY AND CORNBREAD

1 2½-lb	turkey breast
	salt and pepper
6 sprigs	rosemary
6 sprigs	thyme
6 sprigs	parsley
2 cloves	garlic, peeled and thinly slices
	olive oil for grilling
6	thick slices of cornbread
	butter softened
	mango chutney

Lift the edge of the skin carefully from the turkey on both sides of the breast, creating a pocket under the skin. Sprinkle the inside of the pocket with salt and pepper, then add a few sprigs of each herb and some slices of garlic. Brush the turkey breast with olive oil and place on one side of the grill over moderately high heat. Turn the burner under the turkey off and close the barbecue lid. Cook, basting with olive oil, and turning until the turkey has turned a nice golden brown on the outside and is no longer pink on the inside, about 60 to 90 minutes.

Toast the cornbread slices on the grill over moderate heat until golden on both sides. Butter and serve with mango chutney. Serves 6.

Mango Chutney

3	mangos, pitted, peeled, and cut in ½-inch dice
1	papaya, peeled, seeded, and cut in ½-inch dice
1	onion, peeled and finely chopped
1	green pepper, seeded and cut in ½-inch dice
¼ cup	crystallized ginger, finely chopped
2 cloves	garlic, minced
1	lime, cut in ¼-inch dice
½ cup	seeded raisins
½ cup	golden raisins
1½ cups	brown sugar
1½ cups	white wine vinegar
½ cup	white balsamic vinegar
2 tsp	cinnamon
½ tsp	cloves
½ tsp	allspice
¼ tsp	cayenne
1 tsp	salt

Combine all the ingredients in a large stainless steel stock pot and bring to a boil over high heat, stirring constantly. Reduce the heat and simmer, stirring occasionally, until the chutney reaches the desired consistency, 1 to 2 hours. Pack into sterilized jars and seal. Makes 4 jars of chutney.

CORNBREAD

1½ cups	yellow cornmeal
1 cup	flour
½ cup	sugar
1 tbsp	baking powder
1 tsp	salt
1½ cups	milk
¾ cup	butter, melted
2	eggs, lightly beaten
	butter for the loaf pan

Combine the cornmeal, flour, sugar, baking powder, and salt in a bowl. Combine the milk and butter in another bowl, then stir to cool the butter. Add the eggs. Stir well. Add the liquid ingredients to the dry ingredients and stir to combine, using as few strokes as possible. Pour the batter into a well-buttered loaf pan and place in a 400°F oven. Bake until a cake tester inserted into the middle of the loaf comes out clean, 40 to 60 minutes. Cool on a rack for a few minutes before removing from the pan. Cool before grilling. Makes 1 loaf.

MARMALADE CURRY CHICKEN

⅓ cup	marmalade
2 tbsp	olive oil
2 tbsp	white wine vinegar
1 clove	garlic, peeled and crushed
1 tbsp	curry powder
12	boneless, skinless chicken breast halves
1	navel orange cut into 6 wedges (for garnish)

Combine marmalade, olive oil, white wine vinegar, garlic, curry powder, then add the chicken breasts. Marinate for 1 hour at room temperature or longer in a refrigerator. Grill the chicken over high heat, brushing with the marinade, and turning until the outside is nicely glazed and the inside is no longer pink. Serve with orange wedges. Serves 6.

Pheasant Breasts with Mushroom Port Sauce

½ cup	dried currants
1 cup	port
¼ cup	olive oil
¼ lb	fresh mushrooms, sliced
½	red onion, peeled and minced
3 cups	chicken stock
2 tbsp	butter
2 tbsp	flour
	salt and pepper
4	pheasant breasts
	olive oil for grilling
	salt and pepper

Put the currants in a small bowl and add the port. Let stand at least 2 hours or overnight. Drain the currants, reserving the liquid.

Heat the olive oil in a medium skillet over moderate heat on the side burner of the barbecue. Add the mushrooms and shallots, and cook until the mushroom liquid has mostly evaporated and the onions are softened. Add the chicken stock and currants, and cook until the mixture is reduced to about ½ cup. Add the port from the currants and reduce a little again, about 5 more minutes. Mash the butter and flour together until they form a paste. Blend in a little sauce and then add the mixture to the pan. Stir and cook until heated through, about 1 minute. Season with salt and pepper. Cover and keep warm.

Meanwhile, brush the pheasant breasts with olive oil, season with salt and pepper, and place on one side of the barbecue over moderately high heat. Cook, turning and basting until the pheasant is no longer pink on the inside, about 30 minutes or so. Pierce the pheasant with a skewer. If the juices run clear, it is done. If they run pink, cook it a little longer. Serve in a pool of sauce. Serves 4.

Pineapple Chicken

½ cup	pineapple juice
¼ cup	brown sugar
1 tsp	fresh ginger, grated
¼ cup	soya sauce
2 cloves	garlic, peeled and crushed
2 tbsp	olive oil
12	boneless chicken breast halves
1	whole fresh pineapple

Combine pineapple juice, brown sugar, ginger, soya sauce, garlic, and olive oil in a dish, then add the chicken breasts. Marinate for about one hour at room temperature or overnight in the refrigerator. Trim the foliage and outer skin from the pineapple and cut into 8 long wedges, removing the hard inner core from each wedge. Cook the chicken over high heat, along with the pineapple wedges, brushing and turning as needed until nicely browned on the outside, and no longer pink on the inside. Serves 6.

SALADS

Alison's Chicken and Shrimp Rice Stick Noodle Salad

½ 227-gram	package of rice stick noodles
	boiling water
1	yellow pepper
3 tbsp	canola oil
1 tsp	ground ginger
2	skinless, boneless chicken breasts
12	shrimp, peeled
1	avocado, peeled, pitted, and cut in 1-inch dice
3 tbsp	grated coconut
¼ cup	cilantro
2 tbsp	canola oil
2 tsp	soy sauce
4 tsp	rice wine vinegar
2 tbsp	fresh lime juice
½ tsp	ground ginger
½–1 tsp	Wasabi mustard
½ cup	salted peanuts, chopped

Place noodles in a large heat-proof bowl. Add boiling water to cover. Soak for 10 minutes. Drain and rinse under cold water.

Put the pepper on the grill over high heat and cook on four sides until completely blackened. Place it in a paper bag to sweat for 5 minutes. Rub the skin from the pepper, cut in half, and seed. Cut the pepper into 1-inch pieces.

Combine the canola oil and ginger, and then coat the chicken and shrimp with it. Put the shrimp on skewers.

Place the shrimp and chicken on the grill over high heat. Cook until the shrimp curl and turn pink, and the chicken is no longer pink on the inside. Remove the tails from the shrimp and cut the shrimp in half lengthwise. Cut the chicken lengthwise into ¼-inch slices, then cut in half.

Put the noodles, yellow pepper, chicken, and shrimp in a bowl, then add the avocado, coconut, and cilantro. Combine the canola oil, soy sauce, rice wine vinegar, lime juice, ginger, and Wasabi mustard. Combine well and pour over the salad. Toss well and serve. Pass the peanuts for garnishing separately to avoid any allergic reaction. Serves 4.

Amy and Alison's Steak and Mango Pasta Salad

1 strip	loin steak
	salt and pepper
4	potatoes, cut in 1-inch dice
2 tbsp	olive oil
	salt and pepper
1 cup	sugar snap peas
½ package	fusilli pasta
1	mango, cut in 1-inch sections and then cut from the peel
¼ cup	lime juice
½	jalepeño pepper
½ cup	fresh cilantro, minced
	salt and pepper

Sprinkle the steak with salt and pepper, and place on the grill over high heat. Cook 4 to 5 minutes a side until the inside of the steak is medium rare. Remove from the grill and let stand about 5 minutes. Cut the steak into ¼-inch slices. Set aside and cool to room temperature.

Place the potatoes in a bowl and toss with the olive oil, salt, and pepper. Pour the contents onto a piece of barbecue-strength foil and wrap the potatoes with the edges forming a package. Place on the grill over moderate heat and cook until tender, about 30 to 40 minutes. Set aside.

Blanch the sugar snap peas in boiling, salted water for 1 minute. Dump into a colander and refresh under cold running water. Spread on paper towels to dry.

Combine the steak, potatoes, peas, and mango in a serving bowl. Add the lime juice, jalepeño pepper, cilantro, salt and pepper, and toss well. Serves 4 to 6.

APPLE-WALNUT SALAD WITH CHEDDAR CHEESE

1	Granny Smith apple
1	Royal Gala apple
1	Golden Delicious apple
	canola oil for grilling
1 cup	walnut halves
2 tbsp	butter
1 tsp	honey
8	arugula leaves, torn into pieces
½ cup	old Cheddar cheese, crumbled
2½ tbsp	olive oil
3 tbsp	white balsamic vinegar
1 tbsp	lemon juice
½ tsp	Dijon mustard
	salt and pepper

Cut each apple into eight sections and remove cores. Brush with canola oil and place on the grill immediately over moderately high heat. Brush and turn them until they are nicely browned and tender crisp.

Heat the butter and honey in a small skillet on the side burner over moderate heat. Add the walnut halves and stir to coat. Cook the walnuts until they are golden brown, about 2 minutes. Allow to cool a few minutes.

Assemble the grilled apples, toasted walnuts, watercress, and cheese in a large salad bowl. Combine the olive oil, vinegar, lemon juice, mustard, salt, and pepper in a small jar. Shake well and pour over the salad. Toss and serve. Serves 4 to 6.

Avocado and Chicken Salad

8	boneless, skinless chicken thighs
¼ cup	olive oil
2 cloves	garlic, peeled and minced
2 bunches	asparagus
1 bunch	broccoli
2	avocados, peeled, pitted, and cut in 1-inch dice
4	new potatoes, boiled and cut in 1-inch dice
½ red	onion, peeled and thinly sliced
½ cup	olive oil
¼ cup	white wine vinegar
2 tbsp	lemon juice
1 tsp	Dijon mustard
	salt and pepper

Trim excess fat from the chicken thighs and lay them flat on a work surface. Combine the olive oil and garlic in a small bowl and brush on both sides of the chicken thighs. Place on the grill over high heat and cook on both sides until browned and cooked through, about 3 minutes a side. Cool to room temperature. Cut into 1-inch pieces. Set aside.

Cut the top 2 inches from the asparagus and broccoli, and reserve the stem portions for another use. Blanch the 2 vegetables in their own pots of boiling water for about 30 seconds each. Drain and refresh under cold water.

Put the chicken, asparagus, broccoli, avocados, potatoes, and onion in a serving bowl. Combine the olive oil, vinegar, lemon juice, mustard, salt, and pepper in a small jar with a lid. Shake well, pour over the salad, and toss. Serves 4.

CURRIED CHICKEN SALAD

6	boneless, skinless chicken breast halves
2 tsp	curry powder
	olive oil for grilling
1 head	leaf lettuce or Boston lettuce
1 cup	purple or black seedless grapes
⅔ cup	pecan halves
½ cup	mayonnaise
1 tbsp	curry powder
1–3 tsp	orange juice
1	navel orange

Rub the chicken breasts with the curry powder, brush with olive oil, and grill over high heat, brushing with the oil and turning, until the chicken is browned a little on the outside and no longer pink on the inside. Cut the chicken into bite-size pieces. In a bowl, combine the chicken, grapes, pecans, mayonnaise, and curry powder, then mix well. Add the orange juice to dilute the mayonnaise a little. Arrange several lettuce leaves on 4 salad plates. Heap several spoonfuls of salad onto the lettuce. Cut the stem-end off the orange and then cut in four. Cut each slice to the center, pull the two sides apart, and set on top of the salad. Squeeze a little juice from the ends of the orange over the 4 plates. Serves 4.

Israeli Couscous Beef Salad

2 tbsp	olive oil
2 cloves	garlic, peeled and minced
1 cup	Israeli couscous
	salt and pepper
1 cup	beef stock
1	filet mignon, cut about 1¼ inch thick, barbecued to medium rare
1	tomato, cut in 1-inch dice
½	medium red onion, thinly sliced
4 oz	mushrooms, sliced and browned in 1 tbsp olive oil
2 tbsp	fresh, flat-leaf parsley, minced
2 tbsp	olive oil
4 tbsp	red balsamic vinegar
2 tsp	Dijon mustard
	salt and pepper

Heat the olive oil in a medium saucepan over moderate heat then add the garlic. Cook about 30 seconds before adding the couscous. Cook and stir until the couscous turns slightly brown. Add the salt, pepper, and beef stock. Cover the pot, reduce the heat to low, and simmer for 8 to 10 minutes, stirring occasionally. Remove cover and cool to room temperature.

Place the couscous, steak, tomatoes, onion, mushrooms, and parsley in a serving bowl. Combine the olive oil, balsamic vinegar, mustard, salt, and pepper in a small jar with a lid and shake well. Pour over the salad. Toss. Serves 4.

Lamb Couscous Salad

1 cup	couscous
1 cup	chicken stock
1 tbsp	olive oil
3 cloves	garlic, peeled and minced
2 tbsp	flat leaf parsley
	salt and pepper
1 cup	grilled lamb, cut into 1-inch chunks
½	cucumber, peeled, seeded, and cut in 1-inch chunks
1	tomato, cut in 1-inch chunks
½ cup	raisins
2 tbsp	olive oil
2 tbsp	red balsamic vinegar
1 tbsp	lemon juice
	salt and pepper

Place the couscous in a bowl. Bring the chicken stock to a boil on the side burner of the barbecue over high heat. Pour the stock over the couscous. Stir and then cover with foil. Let stand about 15 minutes. Remove foil and fluff the couscous with a fork. Heat the olive oil in a small skillet on the side burner of the barbecue over moderate heat. Add the garlic and cook until brown, about 1 minute. Pour over the couscous and toss. Add the parsley and toss again. Season with salt and pepper, and cool to room temperature.

Add the lamb, cucumber, tomato, and raisins. Combine the olive oil, balsamic vinegar, lemon juice, and salt and pepper in a small covered container and shake well. Pour over the salad. Toss and serve. Chill the salad before serving. The flavour improves if the salad is allowed to sit for 30 minutes or more. Serves 4.

Lamb Salad with Feta Cheese and Olives

½	boneless leg of lamb
¼ cup	olive oil
2 cloves	garlic, peeled and mashed
1 bunch	watercress
1 cup	black olives
8 oz	feta cheese, crumbled in ½-inch pieces
1 pint	cherry tomatoes
3	scallions, chopped
	pita toasts

Spread the piece of lamb on a flat work surface and pound it with a mallet until the all of the lamb is about the same thickness. Combine the olive oil and garlic, and spread on both sides of the lamb. Place the lamb on the barbecue over high heat and cook, turning as needed, until the outside is browned and the inside is medium rare. Let cool to room temperature. Slice into ¼-inch thick slices and then cut so they are not more than 2 inches long.

Place the lamb in a large bowl. Add the watercress, olives, cheese, tomatoes, and scallions. Combine the olive oil, vinegar, lemon juice, mustard, salt, and pepper. Mix well and pour over the salad ingredients. Toss well and serve with pita toasts. Serves 6.

SALMON WHEAT BERRY SALAD WITH ASIAN DRESSING

3 ½ cups	water
1 cup	wheat berries
4 tbsp	soy sauce
3 tbsp	lime juice
2 tbsp	sesame oil
1 tbsp	red balsamic vinegar
1 tbsp	honey
2	salmon steaks
	olive oil for grilling
	salt and pepper
¼ cup	sesame seeds
1 tbsp	olive oil
¼ cup	pumpkin seeds
	sea salt
2 cups	cherry tomatoes, halved
2 cups	cucumber, cut in 1-inch dice
4 green	onions, green part only, chopped
	salt and pepper

Bring the water to a boil over high heat then add the wheat berries. Let the water return to a boil. Reduce the heat, cover, and simmer until cooked al dente – tender but firm – about 50 to 55 minutes. Cool.

Combine the soy sauce, lime juice, sesame oil, vinegar, and honey. Mix well and pour over the wheat berries. Let stand at room temperature for about 1 hour.

Meanwhile, brush the salmon steaks with olive oil then season with salt and pepper. Place on the grill over high heat and cook, turning as needed, until nicely browned on the outside and opaque throughout. Cool and cut into 1-inch cubes. Add to the wheat berries.

Toast the sesame seeds in a small skillet over high heat until golden. Cool and add to the salad. Put the 1 tbsp olive oil in the skillet over high heat and add the pumpkin seeds. Cook while stirring until the seeds stop popping and have turned brown. Sprinkle with salt.

Add the tomatoes, cucumber, and green onions. Combine the salad ingredients. Season with salt and pepper. Chill and serve. Serves 4.

Scallop Mango and Black Bean Salad with Mango Dressing

¼ cup	olive oil
2 tbsp	lemon juice
2 lbs	sea scallops
2 cans	black beans, rinsed and drained
½	red onion, peeled and thinly sliced
1½	mangos, peeled, pitted, and cut in ½-inch dice
1 pint	grape tomatoes, stemmed and cut in half
	mango dressing

Combine the olive oil and lemon juice, then add the scallops. Toss to coat. Place the scallops in a grill basket on the barbecue over high heat and cook, turning as needed, until they are browned on the outside and just turning opaque on the inside. Cool to room temperature. Place the scallops in a serving bowl and add the beans, onion, mangoes, and grape tomatoes. Toss with the mango dressing and serve. Serves 4.

Mango Dressing

½	mango, peeled, pitted, and chopped
2 tbsp	red onion, peeled and finely chopped
1 tbsp	garlic, peeled and minced
2 tbsp	fresh mint, minced
⅓ cup	lime juice
¾ cup	olive oil
	salt and pepper

Place mango, onion, garlic, mint, and lime juice in a blender or food processor and process until smooth. Add the olive oil in a steady stream with the processor running. Season with salt and pepper.

Shrimp Salad with Chili Lime Dressing

¼ cup	olive oil
1 tbsp	lemon juice
2 lbs	large shrimp, shells removed
3 ears	corn, husked
	olive oil for grilling
	salt and pepper
3 large	navel oranges
3 tbsp	canola oil
2 tbsp	rice wine vinegar
2 tbsp	sesame oil
1 tbsp	lime juice
2 tbsp	orange juice
1 clove	garlic, peeled and minced
½	jalapeño pepper, seeded and minced
2 tsp	fresh ginger, peeled and grated
	salt and pepper
2 bunches	arugula
½ cup	cashews
½	red onion, peeled and thinly sliced
1 can	black beans, drained and rinsed

Combine the olive oil and lemon juice in a large bowl then add the shrimp. Toss to coat. Put the shrimp in a grill basket and set on the barbecue over high heat. Cook the shrimp, brushing and turning as needed, until the shrimp have turned pink and are cooked through, about 3 to 4 minutes. Cool. Trim the tails from the shrimp and cut in half.

Brush the corn with a little olive oil and place on the grill over moderately high heat. Sprinkle with salt and pepper. Brush and turn the corn until it is nicely browned and tender, about 8 minutes. Cool the corn to room temperature. Cut the kernels from the cob.

Using a small sharp knife, trim the peel from the top and bottom of the orange and then the sides. Holding the oranges over a bowl, slice from the edge of the orange into the center and remove the orange segments from between the membranes.

Combine the canola oil, rice wine vinegar, sesame oil, lime juice, orange juice from the bowl of oranges, garlic, jalapeño pepper, ginger, salt, and pepper in a large bowl. Mix well.

Put the orange segments into a large serving bowl. Add the shrimp, corn, arugula, cashews, onion, and black beans. Pour the dressing over the salad, toss and serve. Serves 6.

STEAK AND POTATO SALAD

Any greens can be substituted for the baby spinach. Mesculin Mix greens are readily available these days at supermarkets and arugula would be nice too.

12	baby red potatoes, cut in half
2 tbsp	olive oil
	salt and pepper
2 or 3	filet mignon steaks, about 1¼ inches thick
	olive oil for grilling
	salt and pepper
¼	red onion, peeled and sliced very thinly
2 cups	baby spinach
¼ cup	olive oil
3 tbsp	red balsamic vinegar
1 tsp	Dijon mustard
	salt and pepper

Put the potatoes in a bowl, toss with the 2 tbsp olive oil, and season with salt and pepper. Place in a grill basket and set on one side of the barbecue over moderately high heat. Cook, turning and brushing, until the potatoes are browned and tender when pierced with a fork, about 30 minutes. Place the potatoes in a serving bowl and cool.

Brush the steaks with a little olive oil then season with salt and pepper. Place over high heat on the barbecue. Cook until medium rare. Remove to a platter and let stand, about 5 minutes. Cut into ¼-inch slices. Cool and add to the potatoes. Add the onions and greens.

Combine the olive oil, vinegar, mustard, salt and pepper, and pour over the salad. Toss. Serves 4.

Tuna Bulgur Salad

This salad tastes better if the bulgur has a chance to absorb some of the flavour of the dressing. Therefore, it doesn't hurt to make it ahead of time.

2 cups	bulgur
2 cups	boiling water
2 8-oz	tuna steaks, 1 inch thick
	olive oil for grilling
	salt and pepper
1 bunch	asparagus
2 tsp	butter
2 tsp	olive oil
¾ cup	blanched almonds
	salt
1 cup	red, seedless grapes
½ pint	cherry tomatoes, halved
¾ cup	olive oil
2 tbsp	lemon juice
¼ cup	balsamic vinegar
1 tbsp	fresh thyme leaves, minced
2 cloves	garlic, peeled and minced
	salt and pepper.

Combine the bulgur with the boiling water in a large bowl. Let stand about 30 minutes, until the bulgur is tender. Fluff with a fork. Place the bulgur in a serving bowl and set aside. Chill.

Brush the tuna steaks with olive oil and season with salt and pepper. Place on the barbecue over high heat. Cook until the steaks are browned on the outside, but still pink on the inside, about 3 minutes a side. Remember that the tuna continues to cook as it cools. Cool to room temperature and cut in 1-inch dice. Add to the bulgur.

Cut the top 2 inches off the asparagus and reserve the stems for another use. Blanch the asparagus tips in boiling water for 30 seconds. Drain and refresh under cold water. Dry on paper towels. Add to the bulgur mixture.

Heat the butter and olive oil in a small skillet. Add the almonds and cook until lightly browned. Cool and add to the bulgur mixture. Add the grapes and cherry tomatoes.

Combine the olive oil, lemon juice, vinegar, thyme, garlic, salt, and pepper in a jar with a lid and shake well. Pour the dressing over the salad and toss well. Serves 6.

Vegetable Salad

2	yellow peppers
4	small beets with greens attached
1	zucchini, cut lengthwise in 1-inch slices
2	sweet potatoes, cut lengthwise in 1-inch wedges
2	red onions, stem ends trimmed, peeled, and cut in 8 wedges through the root end
2	Japanese eggplants, cut lengthwise in 1-inch slices
	olive oil for grilling
	salt and pepper
½ cup	black olives
	feta cheese
3 tbsp	red balsamic vinegar
1 tsp	lemon juice
1 tsp	Dijon mustard
	salt and pepper

Place the peppers on the grill over high heat and cook until charred on all sides. Place the peppers in a brown paper bag to sweat for 5 minutes. Rub the skins from the peppers and cut into 1-inch pieces, discarding the seeds and ribs.

Cut the roots and greens from the beets, leaving 1-inch of the stems attached to the beets. Reserve the good-looking leaves. Place the beets in boiling water and cook until fork tender, about 25 to 40 minutes, depending on the size of the beets. Cut the beets into wedges so that they are approximately uniform in size.

Brush the beet, zucchini, sweet potato, red onion, and eggplant wedges and slices with olive oil. Sprinkle with salt and pepper and place on the grill over moderate heat. Cook until crisp tender. Remove to a cutting board and cut into 1-inch dice.

Place the vegetables in a large bowl and add the beet greens, olives, and feta cheese. Combine the balsamic vinegar, lemon juice, Dijon mustard, salt and pepper, and mix well. Pour over the salad and toss. Serves 4.

Sandwiches

ALISON'S PORTOBELLO BURGERS

⅔ cup	dried lentils
2 tbsp	olive oil
½ lb	portobello mushrooms, finely chopped
1½ cups	onion, peeled and minced
4 cloves	garlic, peeled and minced
12 tsp	cumin seeds, ground to a powder
1½ cups	dried bread crumbs
	salt and pepper
½ cup	chopped parsley
6	sesame hamburger buns
6	slices of tomato
12 wedges	of avocado

Add lentils to a large pot of boiling water. Simmer about 30 minutes, until tender. Drain and cool to room temperature.

Melt the olive oil in a skillet over moderate heat on the side burner of the barbecue. Add onions and cook, stirring occasionally until soft, about 5 minutes. Add the garlic and cook a few minutes. Add the mushrooms and cumin, and cook until the mushrooms have browned nicely, about 10 minutes. Remove the pan from the heat. Stir in the bread crumbs and lentils before combining well. Add the seasoning and parsley, and combine again. Chill the mixture for about an hour and then form into 6 patties.

Brush the patties with a little olive oil and place on the grill over high heat. Cook about 4 minutes a side until the patties are heated through and browned somewhat on the outside. Serve on buns with tomato and avocado wedges. Serves 6.

Big Al's Middle East Burgers in Pita Bread

2 slices	whole wheat bread
½ cup	warm water
1¼ lbs	lean ground beef
¼ cup	yogurt
4 cloves	garlic, peeled and minced
¼ cup	fresh coriander, finely chopped
2 tbsp	fresh mint, finely chopped
3 tsp	curry powder
1½ tsp	ground cumin
¼ tsp	ground turmeric
¼ tsp	ground cardamom
	salt
	cayenne pepper
3	pita breads
1	red onion, peeled and cut in 6 slices
2	tomatoes, cut in ½-inch dice
½ cup	cucumber, peeled and cut in ½-inch dice
½ cup	hummus

Place bread in a bowl with the warm water and let stand about 5 minutes. Remove the bread and squeeze out the excess water. Combine the bread, beef, yogurt, garlic, coriander, mint, curry powder, cumin, turmeric, cardamom, salt, and cayenne pepper. Form the mixture into 6 patties. Place on the barbecue over high heat and cook until no longer pink on the inside, 4 to 5 minutes a side, depending on the thickness of the burgers.

Cut the pitas in half. Serve the burgers inside the pitas with onion, tomato, cucumber, and hummus. Serves 6.

CHICKENBURGERS WITH APPLE-ONION CHUTNEY

2 lbs	ground chicken
1	onion, chopped
2 tbsp	fresh sage, finely chopped
6	hamburger buns
	apple-onion chutney

Place the ground chicken in a bowl and add the onion and sage. Combine well. Form into 6 generous-size patties, about ½ inch thick. Refrigerate until ready to use. Grill the burgers over high heat until cooked through and well browned on the outside. Put the burgers into the buns and top with a few spoonfuls of chutney. Serves 6.

Apple-Onion Chutney

5	large cooking apples, cored and chopped
1	onion, peeled and chopped
3 cloves	garlic, peeled and finely chopped
⅓ cup	brown sugar
⅓ cup	wine vinegar
1 cup	apple cider
⅓ cup	raisins
⅓ cup	golden raisins
½ cup	dried cherries
½ cup	dates, chopped
⅓ cup	dried currants
⅓ cup	fresh sage, chopped

Combine apples, onion, garlic, brown sugar, wine vinegar, apple cider, raisins, golden raisins, dried cherries, dates, and dried currants in a large saucepan, then bring to a boil over medium heat. Reduce the heat to low and let simmer about 1 hour until the chutney thickens. Stir in the fresh sage and let simmer a few minutes more. Cool to room temperature and serve. It will keep refrigerated in a large sterile jar with a tight-fitting lid for several months.

CHIPOTLE CHILI BEEF AND TOMATO QUESADILLAS WITH GUACAMOLE

1	chipotle chili in adobo sauce
1 tbsp	olive oil
	salt and pepper
2	beef tenderloin steaks, about 1-inch thick
8	flour tortillas, about 8 inches in diameter
2	tomatoes, cut in ½-inch dice
2 cups	Monterey Jack cheese, grated
	olive oil for grilling
½ cup	sour cream
	guacamole

Mash the chili in a small bowl with the back of a fork and add the olive oil. Combine well. Season the steaks with salt and pepper, brush the chipotle chili mixture on the steaks, and place on the barbecue over high heat. Cook until medium rare, about 4 minutes a side. Remove to a platter to sit for about 5 minutes. Cut into thin slices. Place the tortillas on a work surface. Divide the beef and tomatoes evenly among them. Sprinkle the tortillas with the cheese. Top with the remaining tortillas to make 4 quesadillas. Brush the top with olive oil and place oiled-side down on the barbecue over moderate heat. Cook until the bottom is well-browned. Brush the top of the quesadillas with more oil and turn. Cook until the cheese has melted. Serve with the sour cream and guacamole. Serves 4.

Guacamole

1	avocado, peeled, pitted, and mashed
2 tbsp	lime juice
1	tomato, seeded and cut in ½-inch dice
1 tbsp	fresh cilantro, chopped
	salt and pepper

Combine all the ingredients in a small bowl.

Chipotle Chili Burgers

1 lb	hamburger meat
1	chipotle chili
1 tsp	adobo sauce
¼ cup	mayonnaise
1	tomato, cut into 4 slices
1	small red onion, cut into 4 slices
4	hamburger buns

Form the hamburger meat into 4 patties. Mash the chili with the back of a fork and add the sauce and mayonnaise. Combine well. Grill the hamburger patties over high heat, about 4 minutes a side, until they are barely pink on the inside and nicely browned on the outside. Serve them on buns spread with the chili mayonnaise and topped with tomato and onion. Serves 4.

Caper Aioli

½ cup	mayonnaise
3 tbsp	fresh chives, finely chopped
1½ tbsp	red onion, peeled and minced
1½ tbsp	lemon juice
¼ tsp	hot sauce
2 tbsp	capers
	salt and pepper

Combine the mayonnaise, chives, onion, lemon juice, and hot sauce in a small mixing bowl and stir well. Add the capers, salt, and pepper, and stir again. Chill.

Hot Hamburgers

1 ¼ lb	medium ground beef
2 tsp	Sambal Oelek
1 tbsp	shallots, peeled and minced
1 tsp	Dijon mustard
1 tbsp	fresh parsley, finely chopped
2 tbsp	oil-packed sun-dried tomatoes, finely chopped
	salt and pepper
4	hamburger buns
4 slices	tomato
4 slices	onion
	lettuce leaves
	bottled chili sauce

Combine the ground beef, Sambal Oelek, shallots, mustard, parsley, sun-dried tomatoes, salt, and pepper in a bowl. Mix well and form into 4 patties. Place on the grill over high heat. Cook until browned on both sides and no longer pink on the inside. Serve on hamburger buns with tomato, onion, lettuce, and chili sauce. Serves 4.

Lamb and Eggplant Quesadillas with Chèvre Cheese

This is a great way to use leftover cooked lamb. Substitute it for the tenderloin if you have it.

1	lamb tenderloin
1	Japanese eggplant, stemmed and cut lengthwise in ¼-inch slices
	olive oil for grilling
	salt and pepper
1	red or yellow pepper
	part of a log of chèvre cheese
8	flour tortillas

Brush lamb and eggplant slices with olive oil. Season with salt and pepper, and place on the grill over high heat. Cook lamb until it is browned on the outside, but still pink on the inside. Let cool then slice into ¼-inch medallions. Cook the eggplant slices until browned and tender. Cool and cut into 1-inch pieces. Place the pepper on the grill over high heat and blacken on all sides. Put pepper in a paper bag to sweat for 5 minutes, rub the skins from it, cut in half, remove the seeds, and cut into thin strips.

Place 4 of the tortillas on a work surface. Distribute the lamb, eggplant, peppers, and chèvre cheese among the tortillas, in the desired quantities. Cover with the remaining tortillas. Brush with a little olive oil and place oiled side down on the grill over moderate heat. Cook with the lid of the barbecue down, until the bottom is nicely browned. Brush the top with more olive oil and turn the quesadillas. Cook until the bottom is nicely browned on that side and the cheese has melted inside the quesadillas. Serves 4.

Lobster Quesadillas with Avocado and Tomato Salsa

12 6-inch	soft flour tortillas
1 2-lb	lobster, cooked, meat removed, cut in 1-inch dice
1½ cups	mild cheddar cheese, grated
1	jalapeño pepper, seeded and minced
1	red onion, peeled, halved, and thinly sliced
1 tbsp	fresh thyme leaves
3 tbsp	olive oil
2 cloves	garlic, peeled and mashed
	salt and pepper
	avocado and tomato salsa

Place 6 tortillas on a work surface. Divide the lobster, cheeses, jalapeño pepper, red onion, and cilantro among the tortillas. Place the remaining tortillas on top. Mash the garlic with salt and pepper, and add the olive oil. Brush the mixture on top of the quesadilla and place oiled side down on the barbecue over medium-low heat. Brush the top of the quesadilla with the remaining oil mixture. Cook, with the lid down, until browned on one side, about 4 minutes, and then flip and cook on the other side until it has browned and the cheese has melted. Cut into quarters and serve with salsa. Serves 6.

Steak and Mushroom Quesadillas

1 strip	loin steak
	President's Choice 4-peppercorn steak spice
3 tbsp	butter
1½ tsp	chili powder
½	jalapeño pepper, seeded and minced
3 cloves	garlic, peeled and mashed
1 tsp	fresh oregano, chopped
1	onion, peeled and finely chopped
6 ounces	mushrooms, sliced
¼ cup	cilantro
	salt and pepper
½ cup	Cheddar cheese
½ cup	Monterey Jack cheese
	olive oil for grilling
8	flour tortillas
	avocado and tomato salsa

Sprinkle the steak with the peppercorn steak spice and place on the barbecue over high heat. Cook until the steak is browned on the outside, but still pink on the inside, about 4 minutes a side. Let stand 5 minutes and cut into thin slices.

Melt the butter in a medium skillet over moderately high heat and add the chili powder, jalapeño pepper, garlic, and oregano. Cook for a few minutes, then add the onion and mushrooms. Cook until tender, about 8 minutes. Add the cilantro and season with salt and pepper.

Place 4 tortillas on a flat work surface. Divide the steak slices, mushroom mixture, and cheese among the tortillas. Place the remaining 4 tortillas on top. Brush with olive oil and place oiled side down on the barbecue over moderate heat. Cook for several minutes, until lightly browned. Brush the top with olive oil and turn. Cook until the bottom is nicely browned and the cheese has melted. Serve with the avocado and tomato. Serves 4.

Vegetable Sandwich

2	yellow peppers
1	portobello mushroom, trimmed and cut in ½-inch slices
1	zucchini, cut lengthwise in ¼-inch slices
1	Japanese eggplant, cut lengthwise in ¼-inch slices
1	red onion, peeled and cut in ¼-inch slices
	olive oil for grilling
	salt and pepper
1 tbsp	balsamic vinegar
2 small	baguettes
	chèvre cheese
	Dijon mustard
4 slices	tomato
8	arugula leaves
8	fresh nasturtium leaves
4	fresh nasturtium blossoms
8	fresh basil leaves

Place the yellow peppers on the grill over high heat and cook, turning as needed, until all sides are charred. Place the peppers in a brown paper bag and sweat for 5 minutes. Rub the skins from the peppers, cut in half, and remove the ribs and seeds. Cut the peppers into strips.

Brush the mushroom, zucchini, eggplant, and onion slices with olive oil, sprinkle with salt and pepper, and place on the grill over moderately high heat. Cook until the vegetables are crisp tender. Arrange them with the pepper strips on a platter and sprinkle with the balsamic vinegar.

Cut the baguettes in half lengthwise and then horizontally. Brush the cut side of the baguettes with olive oil and place them, cut side down, on the grill over moderately high heat, trying to keep the tops and bottoms paired up. Remove from the grill as soon as they are lightly toasted. Spread the bottoms with chèvre cheese and the tops with Dijon mustard. Layer the grilled vegetable slices, starting with the pepper halves, on each bottom half. Top each sandwich with a tomato slice, 2 arugula leaves, 2 nasturtium leaves, 1 nasturtium blossom torn into pieces, and 2 basil leaves. Place the top on the sandwich and serve. Serves 4.

VEGETABLES

Brown Sugar Squash

1   squash
            brown sugar
            butter
            salt and pepper

Cut the squash in half and scoop out the seeds. Place the squash cut-side down on a piece of barbecue-strength tin foil and wrap it up. Place it on the barbecue over moderately high heat. Turn off the grill under the foil packets and cook indirectly from the other side. Cook until the squash is tender, about 30 minutes or more, depending on the size of the squash. Scoop the squash out of the skins and place in a bowl. Add the brown sugar and butter, and mix well. Season with salt and pepper. Serves 4 to 8, depending on the size of the squash.

Chili Mushrooms

8 cups	mixed mushrooms, such as oyster, crimini, portobello, shitake, or chanterelles
6 cloves	garlic, peeled
1 tsp	salt
1	chipotle chili in adobo sauce
1	shallot, peeled and finely chopped
½ cup	olive oil
	salt and pepper

Trim the stem ends from the mushrooms, clean the caps with a small brush or dry cloth, and cut into quarters. Mash the garlic with the salt in a mortar with pestle, or with the back of a fork, until it forms a paste. Put the garlic in a large bowl. Mash the chipotle chili with the back of a fork and add to the bowl with the garlic. Stir in the shallots and olive oil. Mix will, add the mushrooms, and toss to coat. Place them in the grill basket, set on the barbecue over high heat. Cook until the mushrooms are nicely browned and cooked through. Season with salt and pepper. Serves 6.

Cinnamon Sweet Potatoes

4	small sweet potatoes, each cut into quarters lengthwise
¼ cup	olive oil
1 tsp	cinnamon
	salt and pepper

Combine the olive oil, cinnamon, salt, and pepper in a dish and toss the pieces of sweet potatoes in it. Place the sweet potatoes over moderately high heat on the barbecue. Cook them, brushing and turning until they are browned on the outside and soft on the inside. Serves 4.

Corn on the Cob with Chili Tomato Butter

1 cup	butter
2	chipotle chilies in adobo sauce
1	oil-packed sun-dried tomato
12 ears	corn, husked
	salt and pepper

Combine the butter, chili, and sun-dried tomatoes in a food processor and blend until almost smooth. Place each cob on a piece of foil. Spread the butter mixture evenly on the corn and sprinkle with salt and pepper. Wrap the corn cobs tightly and place them on the barbecue over moderately high heat. Cook and turn until the corn is tender, about 10 minutes. Serves 8.

Garlic Cauliflower

1 head	cauliflower
8 sprigs	fresh thyme
4 cloves	garlic, peeled and minced
½ cup	olive oil

Trim away the excess foliage from the cauliflower and cut off the florets, trying to maintain a uniform size. Remove the leaves from the thyme stems by pulling the stems between the pinched tips of your finger and thumb. Stuff the leaves and minced garlic into the crevices between the base of each floret and its head. Brush the tops of the cauliflower with olive oil and place top side down on a grill heated to moderately high. Brush the under side of the florets then turn and brush every two or three minutes until the cauliflower is tender, about 20 minutes. Serves 6.

JIMMY'S PARMESAN POTATOES

8	yellow-fleshed, medium-sized potatoes, sliced ¼-inch thick
2 tbsp	butter
¼ cup	olive oil
¼ cup	grated Parmesan cheese
1 tbsp	New York steak spice
	salt and pepper

Combine the ingredients on a sheet of foil, shiny side up and lifted at the edges to contain the oil. Toss to coat. Fold the edges of the foil together to form a package. Place it on another layer of foil and repeat. Place the package on one side of the grill over moderate heat with the burner directly under the potatoes turned off. With the lid of the barbecue down, cook the potatoes until tender, about 30 to 40 minutes. Serves 8.

Maple-Curry Sweet Mama Squash

1	Sweet Mama squash
¼ cup	olive oil
1 tbsp	curry powder
	salt and pepper
2 tbsp	maple syrup
¼ cup	butter
¼ cup	cream
	salt and pepper

Cut the squash in half and remove seeds and fibers. Cut in half again. Combine the olive oil, curry powder, salt and pepper, and mix well. Brush on the squash quarters and place on one side of the grill over moderate heat. Lower barbecue lid and turn off the burner under the squash. Cook, turning on three sides and brushing with marinade every 10 minutes or so until the squash is tender, about 30 minutes, depending on the size of the squash. Add maple syrup to the olive oil marinade and brush the flesh side of the squash with the mixture. Continue to cook the squash with the lid of the barbecue lowered until very tender, about another 10 minutes. Remove squash pulp from the skins and place in a serving bowl. Add the butter, cream, salt and pepper, then mash. Serves 4 to 6, depending on the size of the squash. The squash can be prepared ahead of time and reheated before serving.

Root Vegetables with Rosemary

6	small beets with greens attached
2 cups	baby carrots
2 cups	small parsnips, or large parsnips, cut into 2-inch lengths
3 tbsp	olive oil
1 tbsp	fresh rosemary leaves, minced
	salt and pepper

Cut the greens from the beets, leaving about 1-inch stems. Trim the roots. Place the beets in a medium saucepan with boiling, salted water. Cook until the beets are tender. Drain and cool. Peel the beets, leaving the stems intact, and cut in half. Place the beets, carrots, and parsnips in a bowl. Add the oil, rosemary, salt, and pepper. Toss to coat. Place in a grill basket set on one side of the barbecue over moderately high heat. Close the lid of the barbecue and turn the burner off under the vegetables. Cook, turning and basting as needed, until the vegetables are nicely browned and tender when pierced with a fork, about 20 to 30 minutes. Serves 6.

Spicy Root Vegetables with Chanterelles

The chanterelles can be substituted with any seasonal mushroom.

1	medium celery root
1	large sweet potato
1	large russet potato
2	parsnips
2	carrots
1	large red onion
3 tbsp	olive oil
2 tsp	cinnamon
½ tsp	cloves
½ tsp	nutmeg
2 tbsp	olive oil
12	chanterelle mushrooms
	salt and pepper

Peel and cut the celery root, sweet potato, russet potato, parsnips, and carrots into approximate 1-inch by 2-inch batons. Trim the top off the onion and peel, leaving the root end intact. Cut it into 8 wedges.

Combine the olive oil with the spices in a large bowl. Toss the vegetables in the mixture. Marinate for 30 minutes at room temperature. Place the vegetables in a grill basket on one side of the barbecue over moderately high heat. Turn the heat off under the vegetables and cook indirectly with the lid down. Turn the vegetables as needed and test for doneness after about 20 minutes.

Meanwhile, in a skillet on the side burner over medium heat, heat the olive oil and add the mushrooms. Season with salt and pepper. Cook until they have browned and most of the cooking liquid has evaporated. Combine the mushrooms with the root vegetables, season with salt and pepper, and serve. Serves 8.

Sweet Potatoes with Fennel and Red Onions

Fennel is also called anise.

4	sweet potatoes
1	red onion
1	fennel bulb, with stems and feathery foliage intact
½ cup	olive oil
2 tsp	Dijon mustard
1½ tbsp	fresh fennel foliage, minced
	salt and pepper

Peel the sweet potatoes and cut in half lengthwise. Cut each half into 3 or 4 wedges, so the pieces are about 1 inch wide. Cut the stem end from the red onion, but leave the root end intact. Peel the onions and cut them into halves and then quarters through the stem end. Trim the stalks from the fennel bulbs, cut the bulb in half, and the halves into quarters through the root end. Place the potatoes, onions, and fennel in a bowl. Add the olive oil and mustard, season with salt and pepper, and toss to coat. Put the potatoes, onion, and fennel in a grill basket, and set on the barbecue over moderate heat. Cook, turning and brushing as needed, until well-browned and tender. Add the fresh fennel and serve. Serves 6.

BROILMASTER® PREMIUM GAS GRILLS

A Division of Martin Industries

P.O. Box 128
Florence, Alabama 35631
(256)-767-0330
1-800-255-0403

www.broilmaster.com

**THE MOST DURABLE GRILL
KNOWN TO MAN**